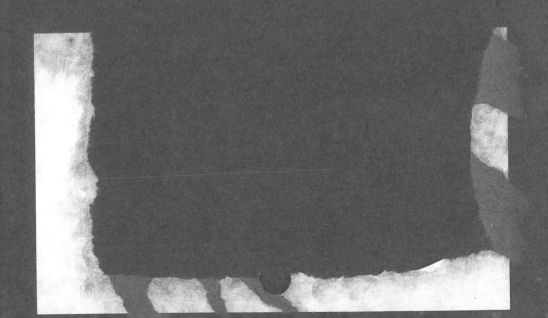

BATTLE DIARY

Dedicated to the members of The Queen's Own Rifles of Canada, past, present and future

BATTLE DIARY

FROM D-DAY AND NORMANDY TO THE ZUIDER ZEE AND VE

CHARLES CROMWELL MARTIN

DCM, MM, CM

Company Sergeant-Major, A Company,
The Queen's Own Rifles of Canada

with

Roy Whitsed

Dundurn Press
Toronto & Oxford

Editor: Judith Turnbull
Printed and bound in Canada by Gagné Printing Ltd., Louiseville, Quebec

The publisher wishes to acknowledge the generous assistance and ongoing support of the **Canada Council**, the **Book Publishing Industry Development Program** of the **Department of Canadian Heritage**, the **Ontario Arts Council**, the **Ontario Publishing Centre** of the **Ministry of Culture, Tourism and Recreation**, and the **Ontario Heritage Foundation**.

Care has been taken to trace the ownership of copyright material used in the text (including the illustrations). The author and publisher welcome any information enabling them to rectify any reference or credit in subsequent editions.

J. Kirk Howard, Publisher

Canadian Cataloguing in Publication Data

Martin, Charles Cromwell, 1918–
          Battle diary : from D-Day and Normandy to the Zuider Zee and VE

ISBN 1-55002-214-8 (bound)
ISBN 1-55002-213-X (pbk.)

1. Martin, Charles Cromwell, 1918– . 2. World War, 1939–1945 –
Personal narratives, Canadian. 3. World War, 1939–1945 – Canada.
4. Canada. Canadian Army. Queen's Own Rifles of Canada –
Biography. I. Title.

D811.M37 1994   940.54'8171   C94–930935-4

Dundurn Press Limited	Dundurn Distribution	Dundurn Press Limited
2181 Queen Street East	73 Maryland Avenue	1823 Lime Walk
Suite 301	Headington, Oxford	P.O. Box 1000
Toronto, Canada	England	Niagara Falls, N.Y.
M4E 1E5	0X3 7AD	U.S.A. 14302-1000

CONTENTS

MAPS

FOREWORD

I was profoundly flattered when Charlie Martin asked me to write the foreword to his excellent account of D-Day and the subsequent actions to April 16, 1944, at Sneek in the Netherlands.

In June 1940 the Queen's Own Rifles of Canada were mobilized at the old University Avenue Armouries and moved to Camp Borden. Rifleman Charles C. Martin, age twenty-one, from a farm in Dixie, Ontario, joined 9 Platoon of A Company. His commander and platoon leader, a youthful second lieutenant, Neil Gordon, remembers him as an enthusiastic, solid and stable young soldier. 9 Platoon soon formed a proud unit, and its members – men like Martin, Shepherd, Hawkins, Oliver and Bettridge – developed friendships that would last all their lives.

The regiment was sent to Newfoundland in July for six months, and there it became an excellent military unit. Then it was back to Canada and Sussex, New Brunswick, to join the new 8th Brigade for further training until the great exodus to England in July 1941.

During the early days in England all of the original 9 Platoon non-commissioned officers (NCOs) – Plewman, Willan, With and Blue – were sent off to officers' training camp. In October Charlie Martin received his well-deserved promotion to corporal.

Training went on and on. In April 1943 I was sent to Africa, a captain at that point, to join the British army for six months of active service. Our 9 Platoon was left to – by then – Sergeant Martin, and we all knew the men were in good hands.

On my return to England the regiment went to Scotland for training in assault landing. From there back to England for more exercises. By now they were well trained and eager to get on with it. Charles C. Martin, ever determined in training and resolute in his objectives, was now our company sergeant-major (CSM) and none deserved the title more.

At last, on June 6, 1944, the regiment landed on the beaches of Normandy. During the many hard-fought months that followed, Charlie Martin received the DCM, MM and CM, all less than enough for the finest fighting soldier I have ever known.

As a great supporter of the Queen's Own, Charlie, may you always stay young at heart.

God bless.

J. Neil Gordon, DSO, CD
Brigadier General

PREFACE

Charlie Martin's *Battle Diary* is the best infantryman's book I have read since Farley Mowat's *And No Birds Sang*. He captures the terror, excitement, weariness and stink of battle in a simple and gripping way. Charlie's words are especially evocative when he describes the intensity of the personal relationships that made the war years the most impressionable of our lives, the fierce loyalty and the very special love among men who have enlisted and trained together, raised hell together and acted as surrogate brothers during the long war years. The regiment was their home, their extended family. This is the loyalty that drove men almost beyond the limits of courage and endurance – and all too many, sadly, forever beyond.

Battle Diary is a record of the personal experiences of Company Sergeant-Major Charlie Martin, DCM, MM, CM, a very distinguished soldier, immensely and affectionately respected by all who served with him. It is a story about real people, told without overdramatization. Charlie's A Company of the Queen's Own Rifles was much like most other infantry companies, and its story is a tribute to all who participated in the war, most of all those young ghosts who shared this special comradeship and who in Charlie's words are "forever young." No veteran will ever forget them.

As well as being an absorbing read, *Battle Diary* is an important book – important because it concerns a critical period in our country's history. Thus, we have another contribution to our legacy of the remarkable role Canada played in the Second World War and of our incredible growth as a nation. It was a just war that had to be fought. The consequences of losing, as we came perilously close to doing, are incalculable. Thanks to over a million very young men like Charlie Martin, and to so very many woman such as his wife Vi, civilized society has been preserved from that frightening consequence.

Barney Danson

(Hon. Barnett J. Danson was minister of national defence from 1976 to 1979; he was honorary lieutenant-colonel, The Queen's Own Rifles of Canada; and he was also the ninety-first soldier to enlist in the regiment, as Rifleman B63591 in June 1940.)

PROLOGUE

A Profile of Charlie Martin and the Times That Were

One day more than fifty years ago, Charlie Martin was finishing a contract for one of the local farmers – clearing ground, picking rocks and using a team of horses and once in a while some dynamite to get about forty acres on Dixie Road ready for ploughing. The Dixie area later became part of the city of Mississauga; back then it was mostly apple orchards and farms, well to the west of Toronto. The horses, heavy grey Percherons, knew the job well, and Charlie at twenty-one was enjoying his work as the land began to show improvement from his effort.

The farmer who employed him was one of the First World War "returned men" – the term of the time – who had come back to his farming life in Toronto Township. He was generally known either as the Colonel or just T.L. – or to old friends and other farmers as Tom Kennedy. The year was 1940; the month was June.

The mood in Canada had become well shaped and focused towards the end of 1939 and had stayed that way into 1940. It was a growing feeling of having to get a piece of work done. The job might be nasty, but another country urgently needed help. This war thing had turned out to be no small business. The 1st Division had shipped out the previous December. Many Canadians had already gone into France through Brest; they had got out the same way. Others had escaped from Dunkirk. Many of the British did not get out at all.

Things had started badly in 1940 and were looking worse. In April Hitler had extended his ring around Europe. Both Denmark and southern Norway were taken. The mood in England changed. The country needed a fighter as its prime minister. On

May 10 Churchill took over, offering nothing but "an ordeal of the most grievous kind" and a "war against a monstrous tyranny." In June it was "we shall fight on the beaches." The words were brave, but not enough.

Lowell Thomas and Movietone newsreels told of mothers in English cities surrendering their children to strangers, rather than risk the bombings. In Ontario classrooms, new faces with English accents – and a few with accents of Czech and other European origins – began to turn up. Many in the United States shared Canada's concern, not so universally in 1940 as later, but significant numbers crossed the border to join up in this business of setting things right.

By June 1940 Charlie had been in Canada for twelve years. His parents, Charles and Margaret Martin, both from Wales, had worked with a travelling circus in England. His mother, unusually adept at matters of clairvoyance, had played the starring role as a psychic and over the years had developed quite a reputation. In 1928 the couple gave all this up and emigrated to Canada, there to take up house building, with some farming thrown in.

Charlie greatly admired both the Colonel and the leader of his local church, Canon George Banks. As a young member of the Anglican Young People's Association (AYPA), Charlie frequently taught Sunday school and helped out with church activities. Banks and Kennedy were both highly regarded for their service in the Great War. To Charlie, his own times in 1940 looked just as fearful and demanding as those earlier days, probably more so. And there was some excitement in the newspapers, headlines announcing that in June the Queen's Own would mobilize in Toronto.

That's how it began, mostly. Charlie lived in Long Branch, working before and after school on 150 acres of the family dairy farm. He attended Port Credit High, and his parents at about that time had gone on to a new farm near London. Charlie had stayed behind – the third child in the family and the oldest boy, with two older sisters and two younger brothers. He was on his own and finishing up on his promise to the Colonel. Now the way to him seemed clear, as it suddenly seemed to thousands of others in Canada. It was time to consider another kind of job. A job that could be pretty important.

The country seemed gripped by a kind of fear, or if not fear, alarm. After the fall of France, England might be next, and after that – what? It was not impossible that a foreign power could approach or even invade Canadian soil. The area's handful of radio stations loved to play the stirring "There'll Always Be an England." In some ways the song was a powerful weapon. Guns, ammunition, vehicles and the other tools of war had yet to be manufactured.

Many who had served in the Great War signed up again. A good number of those who were now too old to qualify for service chose the Veteran's Guard, a force that promised to keep the homeland safe while the younger men were away.

High school teachers – Friday night militiamen – became full-time captains and majors, and if a former student known to be only fifteen or sixteen was spotted among the new recruits, the eye that did the viewing became blind. There was a sense of resolve, a feeling far different from the innocent optimism that had characterized the mobilization in 1914. Nobody expected to be home by Christmas.

So Charlie was not alone in his feelings as he and the team finished up on the forty acres. He said his goodbyes and journeyed to the old Armoury on University Avenue, the good wishes and encouragement from T.L. and Canon Banks ringing in his ears. He was a volunteer among thousands of others in that critical year.

In the months that followed, Charlie proved to be not only a good soldier but also a good student. When special courses came along for recruits, he always took them. It didn't seem to matter what they were. He soon compiled a grab-bag list of credits – knife-fighting, first aid, judo, Russian language, marksmanship. And in his spare time he came close to memorizing his copy of the King's Regulations. This was useful, as it turned out, for those occasions later on when he was called on to represent enlisted men at various courts-martial.

On July 21, 1941, the battalion left for England and the men began training of another kind, initially as defenders of the island, learning anti-invasion tactics and strategies.

In 1942 Charlie was awarded corporal's stripes, and in February 1943 a third stripe. Later in that year he lost his bachelor status, winning the hand of an English girl. He and Vi were married on October 30 at Shoreham by the Sea, near Brighton. Vi was from a small mining village near Newcastle-on-Tyne. Perhaps because her father had been gassed in the first war, she was quick to throw her lot in with this war effort, joining the ATS (Auxiliary Territorial Service). She worked as a radar operator with the Royal Artillery based in London and later on the east coast.

Then 1944. Rumours of an Allied invasion of the Continent were rife as the new year began, though no one was yet sure of it. Charlie became CSM (company sergeant-major) of the battalion's A Company in February. Three months later, on May 25, the planning began for an invasion that would see Charlie Martin on June 6 probably the first Canadian soldier on a D-Day beach. Then seventy-eight days of fierce fighting in Normandy and eight months of tough combat across Europe. He came home to Canada on crutches and, despite an adverse diagnosis, recovered well enough to play football and sports of most any kind. Vi joined him the following year. A picture of them in a warm embrace at Union Station was published in the Toronto *Telegram* on April 13, 1946.

In that same year, Charlie started a job with the Department of Agriculture. His old employer, Colonel T.L. Kennedy, had become the minister of that department. True to form, always seeking to learn and improve, Charlie took courses at the University of Guelph. Later he became a member of the Agricultural Institute of Canada and then a member of the Ontario Institute of Agrologists.

Children came along. Charles Stuart Martin was born in 1947; Richard James in 1950.

In 1949 Charlie and Vi heard about twelve acres for sale on

No. 5 highway in the heart of the old Dixie neighbourhood. They managed to become property owners, operating a post office there along with a general store. Charlie continued working for the Ontario government even though his and Vi's new enterprise took much of his time. It was six long days a week, especially for Vi. The dubious thrill of it all, she says, came at the end of the week when the leftovers in the store's meat counter went straight to the family table. The site now hosts a KFC outlet along with a slew of other developments.

Today Charlie and Vi live in a comfortable penthouse close to the Mississauga Hospital. At the front entrance of the apartment, visitors can't help noticing a framed photo of a young, muscular, grinning Charlie Martin in uniform, posing victoriously on his 1945 crutches. Close by is the framed Orville Fisher print of the Queen's Own landing at Bernières-sur-Mer.

The Martins are long-time members of St. John's Anglican Church and present members of St. Hilary's. There are six grandchildren – Matthew James, Charles Sean, Kenneth David, Ashley Margaret, Richard James and Gavin Charles – and two daughters-in-law (the best, Charlie and Vi claim), Dianne and Candy.

Roy Whitsed

Vi and Charlie Martin

This is not a history of the actions of members of the Queen's Own Rifles of Canada during the Second World War, nor is it a documentary of any sort, nor does it put forward any strategies of battle or opinions about what was or could have been. It is simply a memoir, my recollections about A Company and our assignments from D-Day, June 6, 1944, through to my last battle on April 16, 1945.

There must be errors or omissions. There would have to be. They are not intentional. All riflemen have their memories and sometimes they vary.

These are mine.

Charlie Martin

D-Day: Bernières-sur-Mer (Juno Beach)

A Lonely Landing, an Objective Achieved
June 6, 1944, 03:15 hours to 24:00 hours

Of our Canadian forces, I believe we were the first to set foot on Juno Beach in Normandy.

For us, June 6 began with reveille at 03:15 hours in the Channel. The day before in the assembly area, as we prepared to board the SS *Monowai* from the Royal Piers, Southampton, everything had gone smoothly – no problems, no fear. For at least two years, we'd been training and planning for this; for at least two years the enemy had known we'd be coming. The training and rehearsals were over. This was it. We were among the 156,000 soldiers who would be carried on 4,123 landing craft (LCA) towards our fifty-mile* front.**

We knew that the day's objective for our division of the Queen's Own Rifles of Canada (QOR) was the village of Bernières-sur-Mer.

We had boarded our LCAs slightly before five in the morning. Much has been written about the bad weather during that first week of June. In the face of heavy seas in the Channel, the Allied leadership had surely been in an agony of indecision over whether to go or wait. We knew none of this. But we saw right away that the real thing was nothing like our training exercises. We had practised getting men down the loading nets and into assault boats, but always in calm weather. On this morning the

---

* Imperial, rather than metric, measurements will be used throughout, since this was the measurement used by the Canadian soldier.
** There were a total of 3.5 million Allied troops in southern England; according to a popular story of the time, the invasion "had to be" because England was sinking under the weight of men and equipment.

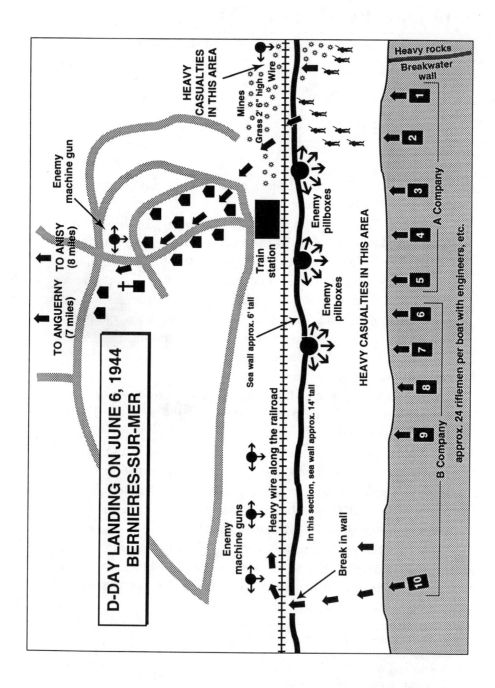

waves were high, and the assault boat – which appeared mighty tiny when you looked down from the deck of the *Monowai* – was tossing around like a cork. Its motor was running but the seas were too much. Ropes held it to the ship, but they had to be loose. So the LCA would yaw and sway maybe ten or fifteen feet from the ship, taking the landing net with it.

Each man had heavy boots and a fifty-pound pack, and some had the extra burden that came with a Bren, a Piat (anti-tank gun), two-inch mortars, ammunition and all the rest of it. One error and he might drop like a stone between the hull of the ship and the LCA. Worse, even if a man in the water did succeed in unloading the extra weight, he could be crushed if the LCA came slamming against the hull.

We managed, but it took time. The *Monowai* crew were getting edgy. They knew there was a schedule to be met. Each of our five boat commanders in A Company was responsible for the loading and for making sure there was no vital equipment missing, so as I was commanding my LCA, I was last in. I went down the net as fast as I could. The LCA had already cast off. When it came to making my jump, I nearly became our first statistic. Buck Hawkins and Jamie McKenzie caught me just in time.

While I was the leader for our boat, the LCA was actually commanded by two Royal Navy men, one a lieutenant, who both sat in the stern on a kind of raised platform so that they could see (but only just) over the bow, which was also the ramp we'd be using. We sat in two rows facing each other. I was in the lead seat. Right across from me sat Jack Simpson, a sergeant and a very close friend. His brother Red was in 7 Platoon. Both brothers were from Toronto. Jack had married just before we went overseas, and now as the next ranking NCO in our boat, he sat there steadily and calmly – nothing ever seemed to get him upset – ready to take over if something happened to me. Above our heads there was a protective metal overhang of about thirty inches.

Ten assault boats were loaded pretty much in the same way. A Company was in boats No. 1 to No. 5; B Company in boats

No. 6 to No. 10. My boat had most of the men from my old original section in 9 Platoon. We had all joined up in 1940, had trained together, had lived together and had just been together every day of the last four years.

There came a one-hour delay. This caused concern, since any delay would mean the assault would be in daylight – which turned out to be the case – instead of just before dawn. But we still had the comfort of the mother ship as our assault boats continued to circle round the *Monowai*. Finally, we turned south towards France. The shore was approximately five miles away, and as we approached it, we could see the rockets and naval guns firing through the night sky. We thought most of this would be softening up our beachhead, but when we got there we would find no signs of bombardment. Our navy guns, in fact, had overshot the beaches. All this heavy stuff should have been a signal to us that there were very strong enemy positions inland.

In the early dawn light, we noticed a single plane overhead. But only briefly. A long-range naval rocket took it out. We were about a mile from shore.

As we moved farther from the mother ship and closer to shore, it came as a shock to realize that the assault fleet just behind us had completely disappeared from view. Suddenly there was just us and an awful lot of ocean, or English Channel if you prefer. Later depictions of D-Day by wartime artists and Hollywood filmmakers would typically show support planes overhead, the Channel crowded with destroyers and battleships, the shore full of assault boats, beach masters and all that kind of thing. Not so with us. All that remained within sight was our own fleet of ten assault craft, moving abreast in the early-morning silence in a gradually extending line facing the shore, the A Company boats on the right and the B Company boats on the left.

Daylight. We had never felt so alone in our lives.

There was mist and rain. Bernières-sur-Mer became visible. Fifteen hundred yards of beach stretched from the far left to the far right. Everything was dead quiet. It could have been a picture postcard of any one of a hundred tiny French beaches with a vil-

lage behind – not the real thing. There wasn't much talk. Earlier
we'd worried a little about the choppy, heaving seas. Now, as we
came closer, it was the strange silence that gripped us. But we
were all confident. There was a job to be done, each seemed to
feel. Let's do it.

Ten boats stretched out over fifteen hundred yards is not really a whole lot of assault force. The boats began to look even
tinier as the gaps widened, with more than the length of a football field between each. Our initial concept of a brave attack
began to seem questionable, though none of us would admit it.
We could see the houses and buildings of the village. In between
the village and the shore were the expected embedded obstacles
and barbed wire with mines attached. In the centre there was a
formidable fifteen-foot wall with three large, heavy, cement pill-
boxes. The entire beach was open to murderous fire from
machine guns positioned for a full 180-degree sweep.

Military art puts forward a different scenario. The assault
boats appear to be very close together and the troops within sight
and sound of one another. This is likely necessary in order to get
all the action into a reasonable frame, but in the actual event it
was quite a different thing.

As our assault craft continued moving forward, B Company's
No. 9 and No. 10 boats headed even further to the left and Peter
Rea's No. 1 boat further to the right; our own No. 2 boat headed
south; both Rea's boat and ours were looking at a breakwater and
some serious-looking rocks on the right. Our first experience of
action under fire started with a nervous gunner in one of the pill-
boxes; he opened fire prematurely and a piece of metal cut Rfn.
Cy Harden on the cheek. The navy chap slapped a bandage on
the wound and said, "If that's the worst you get, you'll be lucky."
He was lucky. Even though later that day an 88 shell landed very
close to him, turning him white as a sheet, he carried on with his
section and survived to handle a concession after the war at
Maple Leaf Stadium. But there were no hot dogs for him this
day.

The crew of two were handling the boat well; that first burst

of machine-gun fire had stopped. The engine purred steadily and
didn't seem to disturb the silence. We got closer. Things might
have been different if we had run into heavy shore guns or enemy
aircraft. The lieutenant came forward to speak to me. We could
see some of our other boats seeming to drift out, not in line at
all, as we got closer. What now?

"Take us in as fast as you can," I ordered. "Don't slow up,
keep us going!" It was better to move directly and at high speed
than to chance drifting as easy targets or broadsiding obstacles or
mines. And I thought the speed would keep the bow higher and
get us as close in to shore as possible. He gave a signal to the
sailor in the stern – go to speed.

Everyone seemed calm and ready. The boat commander was
in charge of this part. He would give our landing order. We waited for it. In just a few inches of water the prow grated onto the
beach.

The order rang out: "Down ramp." The moment the ramp
came down, heavy machine-gun fire broke out from somewhere
back of the seawall. Mortars were dropping all over the beach.
Possibly No. 1 boat on the right took more of the fire.

The men rose, starboard line turning right, port turning left.
I said to Jack, across from me, and to everyone: "Move! Fast!
Don't stop for anything. Go! Go! Go!" We raced down the ramp,
Jack and I side by side, the men closely following. We fanned out
as fast as we could, heading for that sea wall.

None of us really grasped at that point, spread across such a
large beach front, just how thin on the ground we were. Each of
the ten boatloads had become an independent fighting unit.
None had communication with the other, although just before
our touch-down we were all in sight of one another. We were on
our own and in our first action. Every single one of us, from
Elliot Dalton, our commanding officer, who was the leader for
his boat, and the other A Company boat leaders – Jack Pond,
Peter Rea and Dave Owen – to the ordinary soldier, was on the
run and at top speed. We were all riflemen on the assault and
there was nothing ordinary about any of us.

During our training when we reached a beach, we all formed up under our section and platoon commanders with no difficulty. But now we were attacking formidable fortifications in entirely different formations and under machine-gun and mortar fire from all angles. That first rush – racing across the beach, scaling the wall, crossing the open railway line that ran parallel to the beach, all under heavy MG fire – claimed a lot of us in the first minute or two.

The section and platoon commanders were primary targets and fast became casualties. 9 Platoon's Lieut. Peter C. Rea was wounded twice. His NCOs, Charles Smith and Bill Brown, were wounded on the beach. It was low tide and we had a wide expanse to cover. Others in No. 1 were killed in the heavy fire they took – Hugh Rocks (Rocky), who had been such a good lightweight fighter, George Dalzell, Gil May, Hector J. Bruyère, Willie McBride and Tommy Pierce.

Of the men from our boat, Jack Simpson was killed on the beach and Jack Culbertson was wounded. Jamie McKechnie, who only hours earlier had helped grab me into the LCA and doubtless saved my life, was killed and so was Ernie Cunningham and Sammy Hall.

Two men from boat No. 4 came over our way, as we discovered later at the barbed wire. They were Jim Catling and Herman Stock, and somehow their race against the fire found them over near our position. Herman Stock was an Iroquois from the Gibson Reserve near Bala, Ontario. Of course he was nicknamed "Chief" from the day he enlisted back in June 1940. In training and in this action he always led the way.

Our boat had landed about one hundred yards from a section where sand dunes about five to six feet in height had built up in front of the wall. The enemy had been busy reinforcing the defences. As we raced across the beach, we had no time to think much. Our training did that for us. We were men who could run sixty miles with a twenty-five-pound pack, first-class marksmen, about 30 percent in the sniper class, and all of us drilled in the credo of don't stop for anything.

Our part of the beach was clear, but there were mines buried in the sand. On the dead run you just chose the path that looked best. Bert Shepherd, Bill Bettridge* and I were running at top speed and firing from the hip. To our left we spotted a small gap in the wall. It looked like it had been made so that bulldozers could get through to the beach to move obstacles and that sort of thing. They had placed a belt-fed machine gun there as part of the defence and only one man was on it. He was waving his arms furiously, as if calling for others to come up and get on the gun. It would take two to operate it, one to feed the belt and one to do the firing. At that time of the morning they could have been shaving, having breakfast or just generally not ready for some fast-moving assault troops. We knew from our training that you cannot be on the move and fire accurately at the same time. If you stop, you become the target. In any case, Bill did stop for a split second. He took his aim and that seemed to be the bullet that took the gunner out, although Bert and I were firing too. We got to the wall and over it, then raced across the railway line. The marine from our landing craft was with us. When he had tried to get off the beach, the boat had hit a mine and sunk. So he had picked up a rifle and joined us in the assault. Now, as we were about to move farther ahead, he asked if we minded if he left. He felt he should follow his orders, get on another boat and return to the mother ship for more duty. We didn't object.

To both sides of us we had minefields. The machine-gun fire and mortars never let up, a barrage of shelling that seemed to come from everywhere. Once over the railway we had some grass cover, but we ran into heavy barbed wire. Shep and Bill looked a little surprised that we had got this far. Then Shepherd began to get annoyed about wire blocking our way, sort of interfering with his day. We had to decide whether to cut the wire here and move straight ahead to the houses two hundred yards away, or cut the wire to the left or to the right and move in that direction. We

---

* Bill Bettridge came from a farming area in Brampton and Bert Shepherd from a similar location in Etobicoke, just about where the Six Points Plaza is now located.

decided to go straight ahead. (Before reaching that decision, I had checked the sides. We couldn't move through the ditch because they'd strung wire at intervals from the bottom up, almost to the train rails. So I inched my way up and took a look. That's when I saw the Chief and Jim Catling. They were on the rail line, caught by the fire. Jim had one hand on the far rail, as though still trying to drag himself across when life left him.)

There was a brief discussion – necessarily very brief under constant machine-gun and mortar fire – about who should have the wonderful privilege of cutting these heavy strands of barbed wire. Bert Shepherd was the kind of person who, no matter how serious a situation might be, couldn't resist prolonging it with an argument. On that day he threatened to run true to form. He was a fine soldier and a highly qualified sniper (I was the trainer for his group back in England), but this was not the time and place for him to go on and on about how wire cutting was not his specialty, that I was closer, CSMs were paid more, etc., etc. So guess who cut the wire? (Years after the war, Bill and especially Shep enjoyed recounting this episode.)

I cut the strands and bent them back, making an opening just wide enough for a man to belly through. The grass gave us cover. The enemy knew we were somewhere and likely on the move, but they could not pinpoint us. We crept through. By this time there were about fifteen of us.

Then we came to the minefield. In situations like this, the leader gives the signal to cross the minefield and everybody is supposed to start at the same time. I advanced about ten paces and stepped on a jumping mine. When this goes into the air it spreads old nails and buckshot – whatever its makers have put in it – over a large area, maybe 150 or 200 feet. But if you keep your foot on it, it won't go off. So I held my foot in place and got everyone to the far side, over the fence and into the gardens by the houses. To avoid the spray effect you drop to the ground quickly right down beside the mine.

Perhaps I stood a second or two too long on the mine, and as I leaned forward, ready to flop, a bullet somehow hit the inside of my helmet. It spun round and round on the inside and took the helmet right off. I released the mine. It exploded, jumping five feet or so in the air, but I had flattened myself on the ground. Seconds later I leapt up and left the scene, proceeding across the rest of the minefield, with some relief but no helmet, at what you might call top speed.

We took fairly heavy MG fire until we got right into the village of Bernières-sur-Mer. At that point we decided to split up into two sections, but we lacked a second section leader. All the NCOs in our boat had been killed but me. Rfn. Jimmy Sackfield* stepped forward to fill the role and we divided up. Jimmy took his section (Alex Alexander, Steve de Blois, Jack Leather, Ernie Hackett, Geoff Oliver, Sid Willis) around behind the houses. The rest of us (Jimmy Young,** Bill Bettridge, Bert Shepherd, Lindy Lindenas, myself) decided to go straight down the road to the right of the church.

The five of us started out. Bill and Jimmy were on the right, fairly well spaced. The idea was fire and movement, leapfrogging through each other. Three men stay firm – one, three and four, let's say – while two move up to the front. Once they're in position and ready with covering fire, the others come up. Repeated over and over, this would be the pattern for all our advances.

We held up for a moment in a doorway as heavy fire suddenly came in. Again this just seemed to irritate Shepherd. He felt I should know better than to be walking around in full view on the main street. Stepping up to me with his knife, within a split second he had sliced off the part of my sleeve that showed the CSM crown. He said they were concentrating fire on us because of me.

Over the years that Shep and I had soldiered together, he had to put up with me first as a private like himself, then as a corporal, then as a sergeant, and then as CSM. While there was doubtless truth in what he said, this would be his way of scoring points on me when I really couldn't argue too much. Bert Shepherd in war, as in peace, was a character.

---

* Jimmy Sackfield was wounded at Quesnay Wood and died August 11.
** Jimmy Young was killed in action September 17 at Boulogne.

So we moved on. It was about a quarter to nine – less than half an hour since we had hit the beach – when the five of us took our objective, which was the road through the village at its southwest point. Shortly after that Jimmy and his section joined us. They too had got through without a loss. We'd made it, done what we were supposed to do. Everyone seemed somewhere between surprised and puzzled. Now what?

We had not seen anybody else from the beach. In fact, for all of that day I would not see anyone from any of the other three companies, and I would not see our commander, Elliot Dalton, till later that night. Now we thought it best to dig in and adopt a defensive position for the time being.

We found out later that A Company's No. 1 boat just to our right had run into exceptionally heavy mortar and machine-gun fire as it had tried to take cover along the breakwater. You can still see the evidence at this date, almost fifty years later. The fire came from what appeared to be a new emplacement. It wasn't on our maps. The week had given us such bad weather that reconnaissance had been restricted. That's likely why our aerial photos hadn't shown it. There were other signs that the emplacement was new. Maybe they had expected us. Some of the machine guns were clearly freshly dug in, as the earth had just recently been turned over.

At the same time, way over on the left, the men from B Company's outside boats No. 9 and No. 10 found a hole in the wall. They got through and went after the pillboxes from the rear.

But the men from B Company's centre boats ran into heavy fire. They had serious casualties on the beach itself. One of the first to be wounded was their company commander, Charles O. Dalton. He was the older brother by six years of Elliot, our own commander. It was unique in the history of things to have two first-wave assault companies headed by brothers.

Another loss was Freddy Harris, the first Jewish soldier among the D-Day Canadians to fall. Frederick B. Harris, a sergeant, had been one of a group of Toronto boys who had

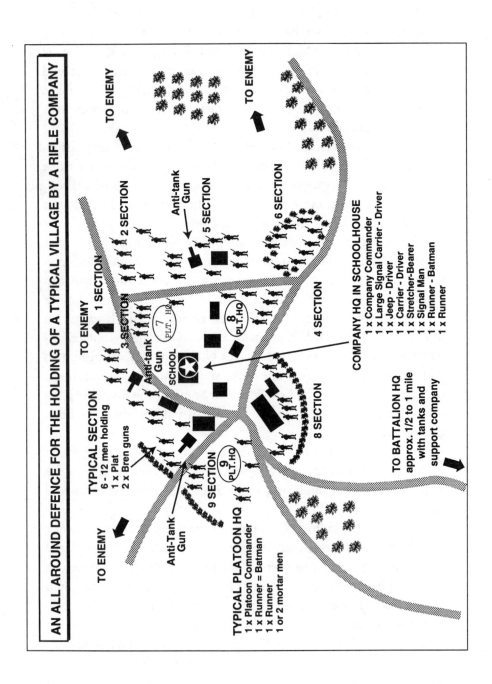

AN ALL AROUND DEFENCE FOR THE HOLDING OF A TYPICAL VILLAGE BY A RIFLE COMPANY

TO ENEMY

TO ENEMY

TO ENEMY

TO ENEMY

2 SECTION

Anti-tank Gun

5 SECTION

6 SECTION

1 SECTION

3 SECTION

7 PLT. HQ

8 PLT. HQ

SCHOOL

Anti-tank Gun

TYPICAL SECTION
6 - 12 men holding
1 x Plat
2 x Bren guns

4 SECTION

8 SECTION

9 SECTION

9 PLT. HQ

Anti-Tank Gun

TYPICAL PLATOON HQ
1 x Platoon Commander
1 x Runner = Batman
1 x Runner
1 or 2 mortar men

COMPANY HQ IN SCHOOLHOUSE
1 x Company Commander
1 x Large Signal Carrier - Driver
1 x Jeep - Driver
1 x Carrier - Driver
1 x Stretcher-Bearer
1 x Signal Man
1 x Runner - Batman
1 x Runner

TO BATTALION HQ
approx. 1/2 to 1 mile
with tanks and
support company

joined the Queen's Own before the war. As things went on, many were called for officer training.* When Harris eventually received his call, he declined. An invasion seemed imminent. D-Day was getting close, and he didn't want to miss it, even if it meant giving up the officer training course. He chose to stay with his unit.

Our small group, holding to the objective, had at that time no notion at all of what was going on with any of the others. We discussed whether we should maybe send a runner back for instructions. Slowly, people from 9 Platoon, some wounded, started to join us. On our left other men began coming forward to take up positions. Within about another half-hour or so, two tanks advanced. One stayed with us and one moved over to 7 Platoon's area. We had started to reassemble.

The problem was that A Company had now suffered over 50 percent casualties and some of the men still with us had been wounded. Nevertheless, we formed up as best we could into two groups. We got the order to move on to the next objective – Anguerny, about seven miles away. As we advanced, we came under MG fire and crossfire from both the left and right flanks. Most of the 88s seemed to be dead ahead.

It must have been about this time that C Company and D Company were landing as the second wave. They were making flanking movements on the objective and soaking up a lot of attention. But they made it with few or no casualties. Without their action, the enemy defence would have been concentrated on us alone.

One tank moved forward with Elliot Dalton,** Jack Pond,*** what was left of 7 Platoon and some survivors from Company

---

* Two of them, Gerry Rayner and Ken McLeod, were lieutenants when they lost their lives at Giberville in July. Another commissioned from the ranks was Barney Danson, who came back to the regiment in August at Grand-Mesnil. He had taken a drop from captain to lieutenant just to get with the battalion and the action. He was evacuated out within days with a bad head wound. His subsequent career would see him as minister of national defence.
** Maj. H.E. Dalton was company commander A Company.
*** Capt. J.L. Pond, A Company.

HQ. The other tank came behind with what was left of 9 Platoon and 8 Platoon, some HQ troops and myself.

We followed the fields, picking out draws, sloughs and low ground when we could. We needed to locate the enemy's machine-gun fire in order to pinpoint our own fire and this was done in erratic bursts of running and flopping, stops and starts, that – while in the end effective – made this kind of advance worse than the beach itself. They had a clear view of us all the time. That their 88s didn't take out the tanks was a happy surprise.

Early in the afternoon, the Queen's Own Rifles captured Anguerny with C and B companies. D Company advanced at the same time to take the village of Anisy. This put D Company a good half mile forward of our position. C Company, then, was given the job of patrolling back and forth between the two points for all of that first night. A Company held the right flank and B Company the left. The rest of the battalion was in the centre of town. In this way we had all-around defence. The Queen's Own Rifles had succeeded in advancing to its D-Day objective almost seven miles inland. We were the only regiment to capture and hold the assigned D-Day objective.

It was on this evening that a moment came when some reality sank in about all the things that had happened during the day. It hurt. We had reached only the edges of Bernières-sur-Mer when we learned that half of our original company – those I had joined up with in June 1940 – had been killed or wounded. And we'd taken still more casualties as we'd gone on to Anguerny.

The tears came. I went behind a wall. So many had been lost. I found myself questioning – idiotically – why war was conducted this way. Four years of training and living together, a common purpose, friends who became brothers – then more than half of us gone. Why didn't they just round up any collection of men in uniform and throw them into this killing machine? Why these, when anyone – somebody else, but not these – could have paid this price in human life? In grief there is not always good sense. It was one of those times. Gradually though, in asking helplessly what we could do, we would find an answer – we could carry on and do our best, that's what.

It began to get dark and the QORs dug in for the night. The support company, the mortars and gun carriers, were holding a defensive position in case there was a counterattack during the night. A good thing.

It turned out D-Day was not quite completed. Sometime before midnight, wild firing broke out and there were shouts and machine-gun fire. A patrol of enemy troops had infiltrated our position. Dealing with them was difficult. This was our first experience with night fighting, and while the enemy knew who and where we were, we didn't know where or what about them. We had to be careful about our targets. A shadow in the dark could be an enemy or it could be one of our own.

After a few minutes we captured four of the enemy soldiers. Three of our group had been wounded. Joe Taylor had been shot twice in the back. One of the enemy SS – it turned out to be the patrol's officer – attacked Frank Mumberson in his slit trench. Frank's bayonet gave him a stomach wound that ended that business, except that because of the narrow three-foot trench, Frank didn't have room to pull his bayonet out. This tended to upset both of them. In fact, we couldn't tell who was shouting louder.

The wounded SS man eventually was sent back to the first-aid post. By then it was pretty close to midnight. We settled back wide awake despite not having had much sleep for the last forty-eight hours. Everyone was very tired, but we still had to be aware of what was going on. C Company regularly sent out patrols to keep contact with D Company's forward position.

In this midnight blackness somebody lit up a smoke. I shouted at him: "Put out that cigarette!" In the darkness I let him know he was lucky to be alive. Then I saw it was the Colonel.* I gave him plain hell. As far as NCOs and senior officers and all that business might go, combat is far different from the parade square. I told him he should be back at Battalion HQ, not up at

---

* Lt.-Col. J.G. (Jock) Spragge.

the front with us – the last line between our forces and the enemy. He was too good and too necessary to be killed or wounded. He gave me one of those looks that anyone who ever knew Jock Spragge would recognize and said, "Charlie, it's such a sad day. We've lost so many good men." He said goodnight and turned away, but not before I saw the tears in his eyes.

Jock Spragge was all man. He was not one of the spit'n'polish professional types, but as a fighter he was the best. To listen to him give instruction at our O Group was a real uplift. This particular incident near midnight on D-Day exemplified one of the problems Canadians in action would face frequently: our officers were too brave. There were many times when platoon or company commanders – and in this case a battalion commander – could not resist the desire to be with the riflemen at the front or even the point, setting aside the principle that the job of a commander is to command.

I walked back to A Company with some heavy thoughts about the Colonel's burden and about the Queen's Own Rifles of Canada, 8th Brigade, 3rd Division, and our landing in Normandy that day. That any of us had survived seemed like a miracle. Later I would find cause to use the word miracle many times.

Despite the painful price, the QOR had managed a successful first day of action. We had landed on very difficult beaches, cleared the village of Bernières-sur-Mer, and advanced to objectives seven or eight miles inland. We had no way at that time of knowing how the rest of 3rd Division had succeeded or what the British or Americans had achieved.

Most of our casualties had been in our first wave, in our two forward companies leading the advance. We had been really fortunate to get off the beach at all. In the landing plan, it had been expected that we would achieve only a fingerhold. Then the second wave would come in to advance past us for a handhold. Then another advance for a foothold. Our progress, then, though costly, was much more than the planners had counted on. It left things reasonably clear for the rest of the regiment to push forward. When D Company landed, for example, they got through without a single casualty.

The Americans were having trouble getting off the beach even on the fifth and sixth waves, we learned later. We of the QOR had some reason to close out our first day with a certain amount of pride, although it was darkened for us all by the very high losses.

Le Mesnil-Patry

A Price to Pay
June 11, 1944

The next move planned for the Queen's Own was to attack and hold the village of Le Mesnil-Patry and to capture the high ground at Cheux. Earlier, when the Regina Rifles had captured Norrey-en-Bessin, it had become obvious that this firm base would be useful in pushing forward to capture Le Mesnil-Patry. But we were a little bit puzzled about the situation. There was a curious scarcity of information, and we wondered what was going on.

The QORs were being asked to push forward seven miles against unknown opposition. We had no information on the enemy. There were none of the usual aerial photographs. There was no opportunity to send out patrols. It made no sense, so the whole idea of this action seemed suspect. At any rate, on June 10 the battle line moved to Neuf Mer and eventually to Norrey-en-Bessin. We were assigned the high ground around Cheux as our objective. D Company moved up on the right flank and A Company on the left to the start area facing Le Mesnil-Patry at about 13:00 hours to be ready to move out at 14:00 hours. There was a fair amount of confusion, which did nothing to reassure any of us.

We moved out approximately on time from our start line at Norrey-en-Bessin. D Company was to move straight ahead to the objective. Our company was to swing towards the south. The men of both companies rode the tanks until suddenly we came under heavy fire.

Riding a tank from village to village for transportation was one thing. That's the way we started the action. But battle was

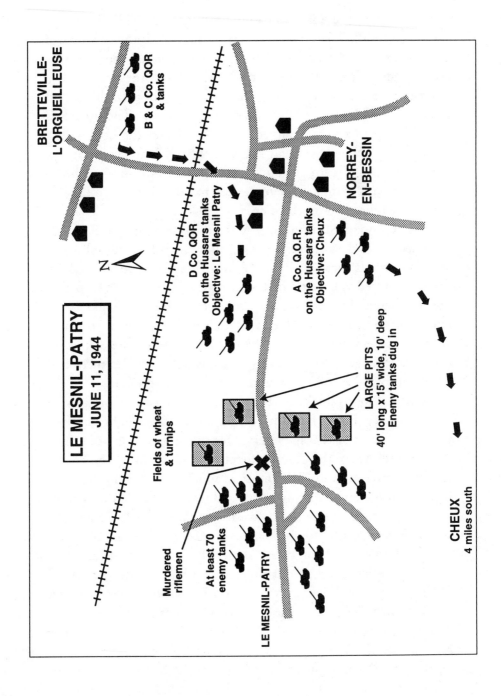

LE MESNIL-PATRY
JUNE 11, 1944

BRETTEVILLE-L'ORGUEILLEUSE

B & C Co. QOR & tanks

NORREY-EN-BESSIN

N

D Co. QOR
on the Hussars tanks
Objective: Le Mesnil Patry

A Co. Q.O.R.
on the Hussars tanks
Objective: Cheux

Fields of wheat
& turnips

LARGE PITS
40' long x 15' wide, 10' deep
Enemy tanks dug in

Murdered
riflemen

At least 70
enemy tanks

LE MESNIL-PATRY

CHEUX
4 miles south

different. Once the 88s opened up, we might as well have tried to ride a wild bull. The tanks sped up, turned abruptly, or worst of all blew up. You'd wonder what there is in a metal monster that could catch fire. Whoever nicknamed a Sherman tank a "Ronson" had a good reason. The enemy gunners could get off three very quick shots within two or three seconds. The three hits would be so successfully aimed you could cover the hole with a dinner plate. Now there was fire everywhere. Hatches came up, tank men struggled to get out – mostly with uniforms on fire – and the drivers with our riflemen tried to put out the flames both in the machines and on the men.

The German 88 mm gun, with its enormous barrel, could have been the most effective gun in the war. It had started life as an anti-aircraft weapon in the African desert. Then somehow they discovered the barrel of the thing could be lowered, so that the gun could be used on the ground to take out tanks or to knock through defences. Neither brick and stone walls nor our armour were any match. The enemy also mounted these guns on their Tiger tanks. Their use this way was the most destructive of all. If you heard an 88 coming in, it was usually too late.

With weapons like these the enemy had our tanks pretty well at their mercy. Firing from dug-in positions about eight hundred yards away, they had easy targets. Our tanks had to get out. The drivers couldn't see the ground directly ahead or under them, so a soldier on the ground had almost as much to fear from his own raging tanks – twisting, speeding up, retreating, flames every-where – as from enemy fire. It wasn't easy for an NCO or an offi-cer to keep some control of the situation in the midst of all this.

The battle raged for a very short while. Within fifteen min-utes the enemy knocked out nineteen tanks. Seventy percent of D Company were killed or wounded. I had given the order to get off the tanks. We were sitting ducks with that kind of exposure and we could move just as fast on foot. Our commander, Major Elliot Dalton, was badly wounded in the leg, probably from the mortar fire. We managed to apply a tourniquet and get him out – back to First Aid. There were other wounded. Some were able to remain in action. In all, the Queen's Own lost eighty-seven killed or wounded; B Squadron of the 1st Hussars lost sixty.

The foregoing is only a very brief summary. The regimental history gives the action at Le Mesnil-Patry almost three pages, calling it "a magnificent attempt to resolve a hopeless situation." An English newspaper report called it "a modern version of the Charge of the Light Brigade." After Le Mesnil-Patry, we took care in advance of any other action to prepare an LOB list – "left out of battle." This, we hoped, would prevent a complete disaster. Those on the list would stay at A Echelon, generally a mile or more in the rear. There would be perhaps our second in command, the company quartermaster and clerk, the two truck drivers, two shoemakers and two cooks – nine people – plus one platoon commander and two others for a total of twelve from the company, generally speaking.

Later in the day we realized there must have been some unusual reason for ordering our attack on Le Mesnil-Patry. The following morning, June 12, things seemed strangely quiet, so in the afternoon we took a patrol into Le Mesnil-Patry – Bill Bettridge, Bert Shepherd, Sid Willis* and myself. We found little except for the dead – the Queen's Own D Company soldiers and the tank men from the Hussars.

But as Bill, Shep and I looked over the ground (Sid was our lookout back at the start point), we discovered enormous dug-in tank positions, curved and ramped pits about forty feet long and ten feet deep. Other tanks had been cleverly camouflaged in the wheat fields. Nobody had reported them. No aerial reconnaissance had revealed them. There could have been as many as a hundred tanks and more light armoured vehicles hidden in this style, marvellous for defensive purposes. The villagers told us there were more than eighty heavies (heavy tanks) along with many, many infantry troops – far too many simply for a holding position. So one thing was clear to us: they were preparing for an attack drive to the beaches.

---

* Rfn. W.E. Willis was killed on August 10 at Quesnay Wood.

Information must have come from some source in France, or from the resistance movement, or from one of our own men behind the enemy line, that a large counterattack was to take place on June 12 from the village of Le Mesnil-Patry.

There is no question that with that kind of force the enemy would have advanced well towards the beach. We would have lost not hundreds of men, but thousands, had we not gone in to break up their position.

It is always easy to criticize the high command – colonels, brigadiers, generals. Many people do it, especially when they are the ones being shot at. But in this case that unidentified somebody in a high position made a most difficult – repeat difficult – decision. I believe this person, whoever he was, knew that he had to commit at least one regiment to break up this concentration of force and thus prevent the certainty of a drive towards the beach. Despite the costs we paid in the action on June 11 – friends dead and wounded everywhere – and the awful aftermath we saw in our patrol the following day, I have to say that any responsible soldier in that commander's position would have made the same difficult but necessary decision.

A battle such as this produces many confused accounts. From my point of view, it was a straightforward plan to capture the high ground around Cheux and the village of Le Mesnil-Patry. Unfortunately, the enemy proved to be highly trained and proficient in defence and far too strong in armour. Nonetheless, our action caused the SS that night to order a withdrawal. When Bill, Shep and I had moved through the village the next day, we found nothing of the enemy. Not a single vehicle, not a single enemy soldier alive or dead. But sadly we could identify plenty of our own from the QOR and the 1st Hussars who had paid the price the day before.

During our approach to the village on that June 12 patrol we came across Tommy McLaughlin* and his section. We'd been crossing through a grain field, following a little dip in the ground not knowing where the enemy was or how soon we were going to hear from them. When you're that tense, every little sound or sighting is magnified. Even at a distance, the six bodies didn't look quite right. We could see the field dressings on the wounds and the prayer books strewn around about. They were around fifty feet from a low wall where the ground dropped away and provided some cover. My guess is they had been machine-gunned in the action and had retreated over the wall to patch up as best they could. I think the enemy had come up to the wall and spotted them; Tommy's section would have been in plain sight and an easy surrender.

Then we came close and saw that each had been pistol-shot in the temple. We had to move on and finish the patrol, but the image of our murdered men in that little draw, wounded and with field dressings, all of them prisoners, their weapons gone, stayed with us. For myself, well, I had pretty strong feelings about what I'd do when I got my chance. But when it came down to it, I couldn't follow through with that kind of revenge.

Our written report was turned in to two lieutenants, Dave Owen and Jack Pond, with a full description of what we'd found, including the murders of Tommy and his men. I expected we'd be contacted for more information, but we never were. We'd lost our commander the day before, and I expect HQ and the Colonel were pretty shaken up about Le Mesnil-Patry, but I always thought it strange that at no time afterwards did anyone ever ask us anything further.*

---

* The report must have been sent on, however. Sgt. T.C. McLaughlin, Cpl. J.E. Cook, Rfn. P. Bullock, Rfn. J. Campbell, Rfn. E.W. Cranfield and Rfn. G.L. Willett were later reported as "murdered whilst unofficial prisoners of war." On December 27, 1945, the commander of the 7th Brigade, Maj.-Gen. H.W. Foster, acting as president of a Canadian Military Court, read the following: "Brigadeführer Kurt Meyer, the Court has found you guilty of the First, Fourth and Fifth Charges in the First Charge Sheet. The sentence of the Court is that you suffer death by being shot." On January 13, 1946, the sentence was commuted to life imprisonment by Maj.-Gen. Chris Vokes.

Bray and Bretteville-l'Orgueilleuse

Reinforcements Arrive
June 12 to July 2, 1944

For the next period we dug in at Bray, holding the village till June 18 while under a strong enemy counterattack. Then we moved to Bretteville-l'Orgueilleuse, which was Brigade HQ. During this time reinforcements had arrived. These men without a doubt were the finest reinforcements anyone could receive. Within a few short days they adapted to the new environment, took part in patrols, and held the line under heavy artillery and mortar fire. They arrived from our holding unit in England and continued in the battle for Normandy with great success, carrying on through the battles for Boulogne, the Scheldt and the Hochwald Forest.

One day while we were at our holding position, continuing our patrols and more or less expecting a counterattack at any time, one of those very human little episodes took place, sort of a bit of home in the midst of war. There were losts of these; this is one.

I was checking our positions and making my rounds when I met Jack, sitting on the edge of his slit trench. I could tell he was upset. We sat together and talked for a while. Then it came out he had had a letter from his wife. The girl had sent it before D-Day to England, and now it had followed us here. Apparently it was one of those unfortunate things that sometimes get set to paper – she'd heard he was running around, having a high time, etc., etc., while she was waiting it out in Canada. Well, she warned him, two could play at that game. And if just by chance she turned up pregnant, nobody could blame her and it would all be Jack's fault.

In cases like this, we always urged a talk with the padre, but Jack seemed to think the only thing was for me to write to his wife. Why he thought I should be the one was beyond me, but that was it and nothing else would do. This was a tough one. To start with, I told Jack to write a letter while I waited. Pretend you never received this last, I said, and just tell her how much you care. This is what he did. I took his letter and the one from his wife over to the padre, Captain Andrew Mowatt. Seemed he thought a letter from me would be a good idea as well, so I put together some words about the rough emotional shape I'd found Jack in that day and how important it was for him to have the support at home.

While I was waiting for Captain Mowatt to censor both letters, the Knights of Columbus canteen pulled up. They had a notice announcing that telegrams could be sent home. And even better, a soldier could send flowers by special arrangement. I was about the first in line and got off a bouquet to Vi* in England. And I got word to more or less everyone at home by sending a wire to Canon Banks,** the rector of two Dixie-area

---

* Vi was astonished to find a huge parcel on her cot in the ATS Nissen hut – orchids, violets, roses – "almost anything you could think of," she says. But what to do with them? The ATS kept things spick and span. She and a friend went to the garbage, found a half-dozen empty Lyle's Golden Syrup tins, took them to "Ablutions" for a washing-up, and set up the six bouquets on the shelf above her cot, where no bric-a-brac was allowed. Next morning at inspection everyone was tense. The officer froze. His eye took in all these unauthorized additions without a flicker. "Martin," he said, "aren't you the one married to the Canadian?"

"Yes, sir."

Then a long pause while the tension mounted.

"Last week I had an anniversary," the officer said, "and I told my wife no flowers would be available."

Vi was sure everything was coming down and that she'd be in for something serious.

"Well," said the officer, finally, "This fellow makes me ashamed of myself. Carry on."

** Through the Knights of Columbus and his good friend Canon Banks, Charlie arranged for flowers on the altar at St. John's every three months in honour of QOR riflemen who had been lost. Canon Banks said a special prayer for each one. Banks had been an artillery sergeant in the first war, had studied for the ministry well after the war, and had accepted his Dixie call in the early 1930s. He was described at that time as "youthful and energetic." He wrote to Charlie every month with news from Dixie and reports on the prayers that had been delivered for the fallen.

churches – St. Peter's Church at Erindale and my own St. John's Church farther east. I knew he'd read my message the following Sunday to both congregations.

Initially, I'd only thought of me and mine for flowers and telegrams. Then a brainwave struck. What about the Jack problem? So I sent flowers to Jack's wife, too. And I did my best at composing a very sentimental note and put Jack's name to it. I never did find out the exact outcome; all I know is that they later had a good-sized family.

The weather turned poor for about a week. The Engineers were having a tough time building harbours, and this led to delays in moving up both supplies and men. Ammunition was in short supply. We were holding our artillery shells, having only enough to repel a single counterattack and we were under orders to use them only if the action was described as a strong attack.

During this time of "holding on," the Allies decided to move a British regiment up to attack. The idea was that the QOR front line would be the British start line. Well, the artillery support dropped a little short, and the Brits took some casualties from their own fire. George Dermody and several of others in A Company took some stretchers into a wheat field, looking for the wounded. We found some men with pretty bad head wounds, got them on stretchers and headed back.

Suddenly a machine gun opened up on us. The stretcher that I was helping to carry got hit. There was a lot of action and turmoil and then I heard some shouts from George. I moved towards him and and when I reached him I found he had an enemy officer in a chokehold. What it actually amounted to was a strap-hold. The officer had a set of binoculars and George had twisted the straps around the fellow's neck and refused to let go, despite a terrible wound in his left arm, with blood pouring out of it.

George was about six two and two hundred pounds and I'm five seven or so.* Anyone could see that he couldn't bleed at that

---

* The enlistment regulation was five eight as a minimum. Charlie had stuffed about a half-inch of newspaper in his shoes to bluff his way up to five eight.

rate and live. So I grabbed hold of him as best I could and dragged him back through the wheat field. Dermody was still using his good right arm to hold his enemy prisoner by the binocular straps. That's the way all three of us got back to the platoon.

I knew that all we were doing was bringing in the wounded, and so my temper was up. I found a British tank and said to the commander, "Follow me – there's a machine gun over to the left that needs to be taken care of." He told me to hop on, but I wasn't going to go for that kind of exposure again. "No way," I said, and repeated, "Follow me."

He must have given me a second look because suddenly he yelled, "Forget it – you've got to get to First Aid." It came to me then how bad I must have looked, covered in George Dermody's blood. I set him straight and it wasn't long before the tank located that machine gun and took it out.

We would be seeing more of these British tanks again soon.

A day or two later, after George had been through the initial first-aid routine and things had settled down a bit, Russ Brough (our assistant jeep driver and company runner) and I took a jeep to the hospital. There were racks on top that you could strap a stretcher to. George was in one, and a British soldier we'd brought in was in the other.

Brough was driving. As we came up from the south to an intersection, we encountered a British column of tanks heading west, probably bound for the coming action at Caen and Carpiquet. A soldier stood at the intersection waving the armour through. Usually this was an MP (military police) and Brough made the mistake of stopping. Without thinking much I asked if he'd mind if we went through. Then I saw that we were talking not to an MP but to the unit's brigadier.

"Impossible. This war's more important than you are."

"But we've got two wounded," I said, "and one of them is yours."

The officer wasn't interested in any more discussion. He just turned away and recommenced his waving. I was in shirt-sleeves, no rank or identity showing. Except for the Smith & Wesson in my belt I was just another ordinary soldier getting an order from an officer who had dismissed our mission as insignificant. I jumped out of the jeep and faced him. My hand was on the pistol butt.

"We're going through whether you like it or not," I said to him. "And you're not going to be of too much use to your lady friends in England if you want to make an argument of it."

He just gaped at me, incredulous. I think he'd always taken for granted that it was not possible for an officer to be spoken to in this fashion. But he seemed to take my threat seriously. His arm came up and he stopped the column. I jumped back in the jeep and said to Brough, "Let's go – fast!"

Just then the Brigadier recovered himself. "What's your name and regiment?" he yelled.

"Charlie Martin, A Company, Queen's Own Canada," I called back to him as Brough dug in the tires and we shot through the column, full throttle.

Some days later I was woken from a sound slumber at a rest area we had moved to. A message had come up from Jock Spragge's headquarters that the Colonel would like to speak with me. It was the adjutant himself who had brought the request, but I wasn't too surprised at that. Possibly a special assignment was in the offing – a patrol somewhere, that kind of thing.

I was told the Colonel was in his tent, and from its doorway I addressed him, confidently enough, "Sir, can I help you?"

He had a visitor with him. In a flash I recognized my friend the Brigadier. Well, the atmosphere didn't seem too unpleasant, though the purpose of the visit was quite clear. They invited me in and offered me a cup of tea or a drink.

I explained to both of them that I knew very well that what Brough and I had done was not in order, but that it was a critical time and if I was to be shot, it didn't seem to make much difference whether it was by the Germans or the British.

Jock Spragge told me afterwards that the English officer had been pretty wound up when he'd first arrived, but that he had settled down rather quickly. I'm pretty sure the Colonel would have had a few things of his own to say – he was good at that kind of thing – and when I left the tent it seemed to me the Brigadier was not too bad a fellow at all. I think he felt the same about me. I hope so.

Nearly thirty years later, Vi and I drove to Saskatchewan to see George, who was the postmaster in his village. He introduced his wife to Vi and me, and then when he tried to say I was the person who had saved his life, he broke down. Both wives started crying and hugging. Tears were streaming out of George and probably I wasn't too steady. All I really remember is that he grabbed me so hard in an enormous bear-hug I thought my ribs would break.

Patrols

The Silent Stalkers of A Company

Even when a regiment was in a holding position such as at Bray, or at an HQ location such as Bretteville, patrols went on all the time. In Normandy alone I took part in more than seventy-five. On some nights, HQ would ask for two or even three individual patrols to be sent out. Some took five, six or even eight hours. The need for complete silence was so great and the stress so over-powering that a man could sweat out five or six pounds. A patrol was as tough as or tougher than any regular attack. The tension didn't let up for a second.

Battalion HQ would send out specific instructions for each patrol. Patrols could serve a variety of purposes: to gather information, to capture a prisoner, to locate enemy positions, or just to keep the enemy off-base and trigger-happy.

According to Hollywood, a patrol might look like an entire platoon. In A Company, though, we thought we could accomplish the mission with less. We developed "the silent patrol." A few men with light weapons – knife, Sten gun, garrotte – were enough to capture a prisoner. Or if the HQ request was for information (the location of an enemy position, for example), again four would be enough but the weapons would include machine guns and grenades. This kind of patrol was useful to draw enemy fire, revealing their position so that HQ could get a compass reading on the precise location.

Regardless of the weapons required or the purpose of a patrol, other units might order a whole section or more for patrol work. In such cases, casualties could be heavy. Our technique called for perhaps only four volunteers, so we wouldn't have that problem. One man stayed at the return point as watchdog; the leader and his number two covered the right flank; number three covered the left and kept an eye out to the rear. We learned all this through trial and error, and always with the use of volunteers. We learned that speed, timing, teamwork and sometimes physical strength were important. The ability to work together in silence was vital. For example, I'd never take along a man who had any sign of a head cold – that's what we meant by total silence. We didn't want to hear a man breathing. We had to be very closely tuned to one another, communicating in the subtlest way – quick and quiet.

Each platoon had some standouts. We always tried to make sure a patrol had some of these. 7 Platoon – the Miners – had George Dermody and Harold Clyne (both corporals) and riflemen Tony Benchorski and Perry McNab. 8 Platoon – the Cabbagetown platoon – had Cpl. Bill Lennox, riflemen Joe Carmichael, Johnny McVicar and Jim McCullough, and Lieut. Jack Boos, who had come to us as a reinforcement. My old group – 9 Platoon, the Farmers – had riflemen Jackie Bland, Bill Bettridge, Bert Shepherd, Wilf Mercer and Buck Hawkins.

A typical information patrol (nighttime) would include perhaps two of these older hands, with one or two others there to gain experience. The critical thing was absolute silence. You had to know how to interpret each other. We invented a silent code, so to speak. On a moonlit night, hand or arm signals could serve to keep someone in sight and to observe ahead, behind and to the flanks. But in darkness a touch on the hand might be the only possible communication. We developed a language for things like: I'm moving ahead, stay with me, stay put, cover me or other such signals.

One or two might stay at the start point; another three would move out about a hundred yards. Extra equipment would include a Bren gun, a stretcher and a roll of white tape. We'd also have a telephone line back to Company HQ. That meant if we ran into trouble we could call for smoke or artillery and mortar fire. Two pistol shots were a signal to the men at our start point to call for a barrage. We would have arranged that possibility in advance with the artillery people, making sure the targets would be to our left and right flanks. But never in front; shells and mortar bombs have a habit of falling short.

Leaving the start point, we'd roll out the white tape as we advanced and pull it back as we returned. This meant if we found our way through the mines on the way out, we'd have the same safe trail coming back. If the enemy opened fire, real problems could develop in darkness. You could easily lose direction. So the tape was our lifeline.

In darkness, time and distance become difficult to read. You could have gone right through the enemy line; they were excellent in deception, camouflage and a whole variety of defensive tricks. Trip wires, for example, could set off a flare. Then there was the danger of panic. It was necessary to train our men to "freeze." Only movement can be seen. A man frozen motionless, particularly if next to a tree, is virtually invisible. Don't flop – unless the enemy opens up. Frozen silent in the ghostly flare, black face, muffled weapon, no helmet – a helmet looks just like a helmet and can cause a rattle – there's every chance a man will not be spotted or will even look to the enemy like a stump or part of the terrain.

In such events, you'd be very glad of the time in daylight that had been spent studying the situation. It was always wise to impress upon your mind, in advance, how the general area appeared in daylight, and to remember it well during the blackness.

A prisoner patrol demanded other skills from our men. In some types of action prisoners might give themselves up fairly easily. But in Normandy the enemy had orders to defend and maintain their position. That meant hard resistance, especially in this type of face-to-face or hand-to-hand combat.

So if we were out to capture a prisoner it meant first of all penetrating the enemy line. We had to take great care in our preparation: running shoes, no loose clothing to catch on anything, dark faces, no identification papers, just dog tags, Sten guns, knives, garrotte and grenades. Our weapons would be wrapped in cloth – no accidental noises.

*9. Platoon. A Co. Queen's Own Rifles of Canada (C.A.S.F.).
C.S.M. (W.O.II) Rowell E.F. — Capt J.E.C. Pangman July 10th/1940.

This is how it began. Our 9 Platoon of A Company is just a few weeks old in July 1940. That's Jack Pangman in the centre as our captain, but strangely our platoon leader, Lieut. Neil Gordon, is not in this photo. I'm in the third row, fourth from the left.

This is A Company in July 1940 in a march-past on University Avenue.

This is a peacetime view of the village of Bernières-sur-Mer. As we approached the beach on D-Day, we felt this is the way it should have looked, but we could see the fortifications and sunken obstacles that destroyed an otherwise very quiet shoreline.

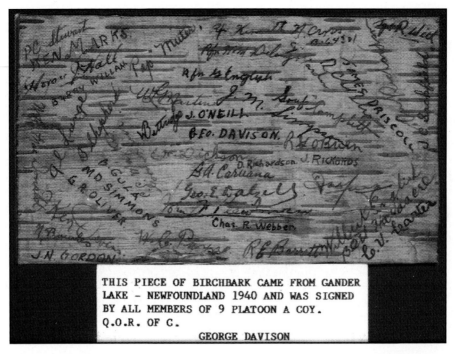

THIS PIECE OF BIRCHBARK CAME FROM GANDER
LAKE – NEWFOUNDLAND 1940 AND WAS SIGNED
BY ALL MEMBERS OF 9 PLATOON A COY.
Q.O.R. OF C.
GEORGE DAVISON

When we had spare time in Newfoundland, some of us – Bert Shepherd, Bill Bettridge and a few others – invented a game. We'd find a tree and stick cigarettes into the bark or in a cleft of the branches. Then we'd move off a hundred yards or so with our Lee Enfields and start shooting. The first one to miss his cigarette dropped out. The remainder kept shooting in turns till the winner was left. The others would have to pay up.

This is how the men came ashore. This photo was taken during training in England.

Another example of how we were trained in fast and well-timed movement. Note the soldier in the foreground manning his Bren. His covering fire would allow troops behind to play their part in a leapfrog advance.

This dreary photo taken in 1952 clearly shows the pillbox emplacement guarding the sea wall. Of course, the steps were added after 1944. Had they been in place on June 6, 1944, no doubt we'd have found them convenient.

Another unhappy view of the pillbox. The remains of one of our landing craft can be seen in front of it. For the marines operating the LCAS, landing was only part of the job. As they tried to back off the beach and return to the mother ship for another load, most of them hit an obstacle or a mine.

Reinforced concrete of this kind is difficult for ground troops to destroy. This pillbox was probably taken out by a naval gun – and a heavy one at that.

United States Defense Audio-Visual Agencies, 72641 AC

June 6, 1944: these are LCIS, landing craft infantry, larger than LCAS, which are designed for assault. These troops are North Nova Scotia Highlanders, along with the Highland Light Infantry of Canada, part of the two reserve brigades that were able to land so quickly behind us on the beach at Bernières-sur-Mer.
National Archives of Canada, PA 122765

Queen's Own vehicles wrecked on the beach at Bernières-sur-Mer on June 6, 1944.
National Archives of Canada, DND 33781

George Dalzell. Everybody liked George. This photo of him was taken in England before the D-Day invasion. He lies buried in France, killed on that first day.

A peacetime view of Bernières-sur-Mer shows the open aspect of the railroad. Of course, the concertina barbed wire we faced is not part of this scene, but the field that was mined and the stone wall surrounding the village are evident.

This is the church where our section took the roadway and moved ahead while Jimmy Sackfield took another section behind the houses. The church had another significance for us when the garden area in front became a temporary burial ground for our fallen.

As we took cover in our ditch just over the railway line, we faced a minefield and a considerable area to cross in order to get to the village perimeter. This view of one of the outermost houses offers a pretty good idea of how things looked to us as we made ready to start cutting wire.

Passing through the village itself we were lucky. This example (rue de la Cordière) shows how it looked. The stone wall (left) was a frequent example of good cover; you never knew what was waiting behind.

It's the afternoon of June 6 and two enemy officers are leading their troops, eventually to a POW camp. There's one of our bulldozers in the background. Very likely it has taken out a part of the sea wall next to the station. It can be seen that the sand has been ramped up to make a roadway.

Photo by Ken Bell, National Archives of Canada, PA 133742

The attack at Le Mesnil-Patry was broken up, but at great cost. This monument is about all that remains, in two languages, of the terrible action that day, June 11, 1944.

"Hurry up and wait" applied to prisoners as well. Here they sit patiently waiting for something to happen. The pillbox behind later acquired a plaque – "To the memory of The Queen's Own Rifles of Canada."
Photo by F.L. Duberville, National Archives of Canada, PA 133754

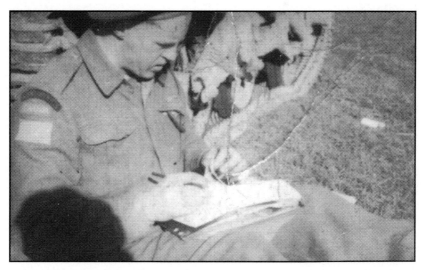

At rest areas soldiers had a chance at last to send a letter home. That's what I'm doing, in the sun with my back against the carrier.

The nursing sisters were always welcomed by a wounded soldier; you didn't need to be wounded, however, to find them attractive. These girls are from the Princess Mary Royal Air Force Nursing Service.
Photo by F.L. Duberville, National Archives of Canada, PA 131426

This is Carpiquet. The hangar buildings were so heavily shelled that only the framework remained. One of our Sherman tanks is in the foreground. The wide areas of level ground so clearly evident here made our action difficult and costly.
Photo by M.M. Dean, National Archives of Canada, PA 131418

Lindy Lindenas, right, and myself, likely around the time we were sharing a slit trench at Grentheville.

Caen, July 10, 1944. The bombings and shelling given to this ancient and beautiful city were murderous. This is more than a month after D-Day, when Montgomery had contemplated the possibility of taking this heavily defended city on day one.

This is the factory area at Colombelles near Caen, pretty well shelled into a ruin. It was here that a wounded enemy soldier – after we had patched him up – pulled a secret pistol and fired into our backs.

Photo by H.G. Aikman, National Archives of Canada, PA 131396

Jimmy Browne, in a photo taken somewhere in England.

Men digging in and camouflaging.
Photo by G.K. Bell, National Archives of Canada, PA 129043

This photo of Falaise does not show the stench and filth of bodies of every kind, but it represents very well the destruction that total war causes to a stubborn, outgunned enemy.
Photo by Ken Bell, National Archives of Canada, PA 132193

Eventually, as the patrol progressed, you'd locate your target – say, two men in a slit trench. Then perfect, patient and silent teamwork is required. All three of us would freeze and wait. As time passes, maybe hours, one of the enemy will move out of the trench – maybe for a stretch, maybe a latrine call. Number two takes him out. At the same time number three moves on the other, still in the trench. Number one man is ready with his Sten gun to cover the situation overall.

It was at this stage that our training back in England became so important to us. Courses in judo, knife fighting and the garrotte proved to be vital to us. Patrols are not for the faint-hearted; a split second and a wrong move can mean death. We were trained to live.

So the actual practice requires that number two moves silently and quickly, knife in hand, on the soldier leaving the trench. The slightest sound will mean death to the patrol. A knife to the man's kidney instantly paralyzes his vocal cords; number two's other hand will catch soundlessly the falling rifle. Then a quick slash across the throat. Number three man, in the same moment, is in the trench guaranteeing a prisoner who will live by the quick use of the garrotte. The enemy soldier loses consciousness without a gasp. Then a fireman's lift and back to the start point.

Prisoner delivered; objective achieved.

If all has gone well, number one has done nothing except stand around with his Sten gun. That's a perfect result because shooting is the last thing we want. This is why a prisoner patrol is the toughest of all, and why a shoot-'em-up draw-fire patrol with Brens, Piats and grenades is something of a contrast.

A draw-fire patrol would include the same dress style, customary with all patrols, plus a Piat gun, three or four bombs and the Bren with four to six magazines. Using our white tape in the regular fashion we'd move in as close as possible and locate one or two positions. Then speed, teamwork and timing would come into play. At the arranged signal, number one would fire the Piat gun, number two would open up with the Bren, and number three would throw the bombs. There would have been a prearrangement with artillery for their part to follow right away, with a lay-down of smoke enabling us to follow our tape and get out unseen.

If everything went according to plan, three men could cause an awful fuss this way, inflict casualties and make the enemy open up with everything. Often the enemy might think a major assault was under way, and their firing would give HQ all the bearings they needed.

My choice for effective results was the daylight patrol. The movement had to be not only silent but concealed. But much more accurate information could be obtained. This is exactly what should have been done in the days before Le Mesnil-Patry. If you're sent out, for example, to "see what you can find," you keep going till you find something. At Le Mesnil-Patry that would have been contact with an enemy in strength in the fields in front of the village. We might have lost some of the patrol – unless they were lucky and good – but against what we lost in the actual action, the price would have been worth it.

In the built-up areas such as villages, patrols take a different approach. Defences are different. You'd find slit trenches in gardens, parks and lawns. Tanks could be concealed within buildings. In these cases, one man at a time is on the move, covered by the others, with grenades always at the ready.

Whatever the style, purpose or location of a patrol, no value is produced unless there is a precise report delivered back to the company headquarters – and fast. At O Group when the attack plan was laid out, Boss Medland* would always ask if everything fit into the known factors. If something seemed out of whack, the patrol leader or a patrol member had to be forthright enough to speak up. Company commanders should always doublecheck a plan to be sure of an accurate fit.

A strange thing about patrols was that they produced men from all ranks who had a natural instinct for the work. Some could move like a ghost – one moment he'd be there; next

---

* Major Richard D. Medland.

moment, gone. Among the best I knew were Jack Boos (a lieu-tenant), George Dermody (a corporal), Jack Lennox, Bill Bettridge (who later moved to a sniper unit and became a sergeant) and Bert Shepherd (Bert later was also a sergeant). It's very difficult to explain the stress and difficulties of a patrol, but these men among others would understand the tension, the silence, the quickness, the instinct and the objective – and how to get out afterwards.

Harold Clyne was another good, tough, all-round man and a great friend. He and I shared an interesting patrol that certainly illustrates the use of patience. This was sometime after June 12 and the action at Le Mesnil-Patry when we were in our holding position. A holding position, of course, is always under some fire, but in this case we were angered by it more than usual. An enemy sniper had wounded several of our riflemen. He was nested somewhere in the hedgerows or in one of the buildings of this small village. But we couldn't spot him. I knew the general area and could tell from his fire that he must be at about four hundred yards. I decided to take him out. Harold would come with me with his telescope. It takes two – one to spot the larger target with the telescope and a rifleman to sight, adjust, aim and keep the precise target more or less in view through telescopic sights mounted on one of our regular .303 rifles.

About two o'clock in the morning we moved out 250 yards or so, which put us nicely 100 to 150 yards from our target area. We made a blind and a small trench with some cover. We were in some kind of cabbage field. You must be very careful in digging your slit trench to distribute the dirt along the cabbage rows so that when daytime arrives, it will not look new or freshly dug. And the trench must not disturb the crop. Under the hot sun, uprooted cabbages would dry out and change colour. It would not take an enemy long to spot the change and to realize some-one had dug in. Since we were so close to them, you can imagine we took a lot of care with our digging that night.

From dawn to the following dusk, we had to stay completely hidden – no movement, no talking, no coughing, because sound carries so easily. The sniper had a partner and we located them both about noon. Two enemy soldiers meant two shots from us, which doubles for us the chance of being spotted. I would have to fire once at the sniper, then cock and aim again at the partner while Harold, with the telescope, would try to guide me to him. Well, to give ourselves a break as far as getting away, we decided to wait till just before dusk.

Harold was on the telescope and I had the rifle. Two rounds got them both. We were lucky; had the enemy observer been on the job with his own telescope, he would have spotted us immediately. Harold had done his job perfectly. You need an observer who can tell you exactly where you've hit the first time, then guide you successfully and very quickly for the second shot. It is difficult, but we did it.

The enemy reacted immediately. They apparently thought somebody back at our front line was getting rambunctious, so they opened up on our people with everything they had. Our fellows poured the same back at them. Harold and I had to spend about three hours under a two-way umbrella of this stuff before we could get out. Luckily, nothing fell short.

I wouldn't want to calculate the cost of all the shells and ammo the enemy and the Queen's Own exchanged that day. And all because of a couple of .303 bullets and two guys dug into a cabbage field.

Battle for Carpiquet Airport

Five Days of Bombardment
July 4 to July 9, 1944

The battle for Carpiquet with its airfield was the next objective. The airfield was an important preliminary in the capture of Caen and the area we needed to consolidate before we could move on to Falaise. A strong armoured division faced the British and Canadian forces. On July 3 the troops moved up to the village of Marcelet. The Régiment de la Chaudière and the Royal Winnipeg Rifles were with us.

By July 4 a part of the airfield had been won by the QOR. In the subsequent action, A Company moved up on the right of the Winnipegs; we were to take the ground and some of the buildings in the northeast corner.

We moved forward under fire, and the men started to fall. Surprisingly none were killed. Then the order came to hold. There are stories that the attack was in actual fact postponed. Not quite true; it was halted. The Winnipegs had dropped back, but the QOR had already captured some ground and buildings. So the order we received was to hold.

It was terrible. We had to dig in along the runway and in part of an old hanger building. The enemy were watching every move from a slightly higher level. At best it's difficult crossing open ground, but the terrain surrounding an airport is about as level as can be found anywhere.

At any rate for five days we took their artillery, the 88s, the Moaning Minnies (rockets) and the machine-gun fire. The enemy were well skilled in firing artillery and mortars. Having recently retreated from this particular area, they could now pinpoint their targets effectively. They had heavy artillery and dug-in Tiger tanks on the higher ground.

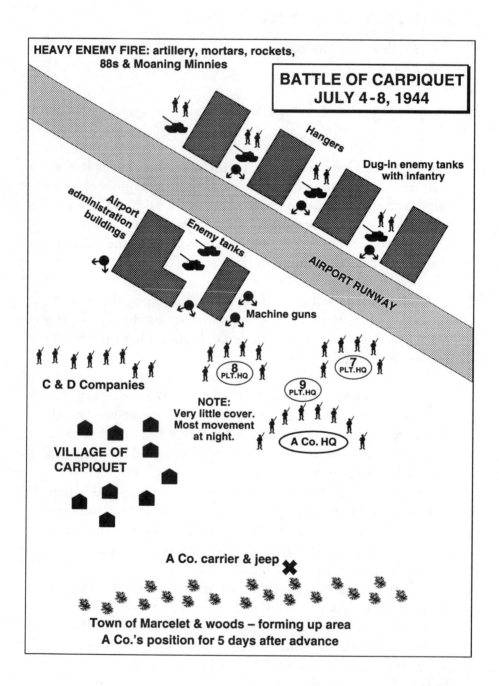

Our assault plan used the battle tactics we knew so well: sections led the advance, one after the other. The imperative thing for each section was not to stop but to move forward under covering fire that came from the supporting rear section. Then to dig in and pour on the fire to the enemy while the next section came leapfrogging up to a new forward line.

When the order to hold came in, we already had four sections fairly well forward: on the east, No. 4 with Rfn. Bill Lennox; on the west, No. 1 under Cpl. Len Hickman; and in the centre, No. 2 under Rfn. Frank Mumberson and No. 3 under Cpl. Norm Slack. They had achieved a front of about 350 yards, and to hold this ground they were all dug in with the point men forward, each section occupying their ground more or less like an arrowhead, with strength dug in on each side of the point and strongest at the rear line.

Further back on the west, we had 7 Platoon HQ under Lieut. Jack Pond and Sgt. Jimmy Browne. On the east, 8 Platoon HQ was under Lieut. Jack Boos and Sgt. Art Overholt. Behind the two platoon HQs we had Dick Medland at A Company headquarters with signalmen, runners and first-aid men. And of course further south again, Battalion HQ.

Five days like this, taking everything the enemy could push at us, were pretty bad on everybody's nerves. One of the first-aid men got so frazzled he wanted a transfer so he could "get out and kill a few of those so-and-so's."

And then there was Charlie O'Brien. He was helping someone get some material to cover his slit trench when for his trouble he was knocked down by a shell blast. Art Overholt went out to lend a hand. The enemy spotted all this movement and sent over the Moaning Minnies. Art sensibly ran for his trench and wound up with his own bayonet stuck in his thigh. Those rockets could put the fear of death into anyone.

As I said, these objectives – Carpiquet and the adjacent city of Caen – had to be taken so we could proceed with the Falaise action and the link-up with U.S. forces. The final attacks came on July 8 and 9, preceded by an air raid on Caen July 7 from hundreds of Allied planes.

The Caen bombing seemed to open the door for our final attacks. The ground assaults took Caen on July 8 and 9 and ours took Carpiquet at the same time. I know civilians sometimes interpret bombing as brutal and unnecessary. But the Caen bombing saved soldiers lives, and in war there is only one answer – destruction and death to the enemy in order to preserve the lives of our own.

We dug in and held out once again at Carpiquet. It meant staying in the ground under enormous fire, but we maintained our position for three more days. One consequence was that the Americans could now move forward more freely on the right. Another was that we were ready to commence action at the south eastern part of Caen at Colombelles, preparing with the British to free up the road south to Falaise and close the gap.

In our Carpiquet action, seventy Queen's Own soldiers were killed or wounded. Frank Mumberson lost his arm in the final assault. Frank, the D-Day veteran who met his first face-to-face enemy soldier in his slit trench on June 6, then survived four weeks of steady action – and with four years of training behind him – was out of action. He rode back on the carrier with the stump wrapped in a field dressing, smoking a cigar, shouting: "See you in Blighty!"

The Queen's Own Rifles of Canada had just completed about five weeks of action attacking a heavy enemy force. Every section, platoon and company – and all supporting troops – had done a job that Canadians could be proud of. We felt we had not let down the Canadian troops who were doing their part of the job in Italy.

In-ground Living

Foxholes and Slit Trenches

Our number-one priority was making a hole. In our training days, we all had the small trenching tool most people have seen in photographs or films. It was useless. Within hours after D-Day, every second man had a regular round-bladed shovel; one in every section had a pickaxe. Two men could make a decent place for themselves in about an hour.

In training, we'd been content with a nice enough six-foot trench, three feet wide and three feet deep. After D-Day, we learned to be more exotic. In fact, there was some competition to see who could create the most elegant trench. So you'd find in some of them such valuable comforts as mattresses, blankets and other household items that served to make in-ground living a little better. All these things would have come from farmhouses. But the men claimed the objects were lost. They had simply found them. Another development was the roof. We found that if we were under fire, it was better to build a trench in an L shape and to roof over the longer part.

Making the roof took us another step beyond the simple foxhole. You could make a good roof using doors from barns or houses. Sheet metal could do the job. There were also knocked-down trees that were put to good use. Then the whole roof was covered with dirt, and the mattress and blankets suddenly had "a room of their own." In the small and exposed part of the L we might have a Bren or a Piat. One man was always on watch; the other could take a rest.

All this digging and construction required camouflage. The roof could not look like a roof and the excavated dirt could not look like dirt. This required some ingenuity. If you left anything around to advertise your spot, it wouldn't be long before the enemy sent his calling card.

As might be expected, the men from Geraldton in the Miners Platoon (7) built solid, effective slit trenches. But the men in 8 and 9 seemed to have a taste for elegance; some of their products were unbelievable for comfort, and yet the camouflage was so perfect you'd have trouble finding them.

For example, Ernie Hackett and Alex Alexander (9 Platoon) put together a hiding place so skilfully that when the tanks of the British 3rd Division were moving through us, one of their tanks parked himself right on top. Although very successful as a well-crafted trench, this cleverly contrived foxhole could backfire. Our men knew what the consequences would have been had this been a hostile tank and had their position been identified; the enemy had a nasty knack of spinning the tank on one tread, mashing down the sides of a trench and burying the occupants alive.

Another time when we knew we were going to hole up for a few days, Joey Carmichael and Bill Lennox gave themselves a deluxe treatment. They had one room for sleeping, one room as a kitchen and a specially well constructed lookout so they could watch without being seen. They even pinned draperies on the sides to hide the dirt walls.

And each trench would have ingenious defences like trip wires four feet off the ground with hand grenades attached, or a telephone line back to A Company, or cowbells strung in a line, or converted tin cans meant to behave as cowbells.

The competition for the finest in trenches was fierce. During the five days of shelling at Carpiquet, where our exposure was very serious, the men developed some Class A models. It's too bad we had no time for photographs. You needed tools of course. And we had axes in the carrier. Dick Klintworth had one on the jeep. It was always one of our objectives to get the carrier and the jeep as close to Company HQ as possible. They were our supply vehicles – first for bringing materials forward and then for transporting the wounded back to first aid.

If we were in a holding position, there was generally not

much problem with all of this. Our rule was protection first, readiness for a counterattack next. After that came food and then cleanliness. In a safe area, a latrine would be built, although some like Bill Lennox, Joey, Ernie and Alex could be pretty clever in their own way about inventing unique locations and methods for taking care of such matters.

Despite what anyone could do to make a trench safer, and perhaps a little more bearable, the shelling could still destroy the nerves. To provide some relief, I always had the men out periodically to move about, make a washroom call, get a break. Sometimes if the shelling was steady and the position well forward, we would need a "get out" trench – more like a ditch – so you could belly your way to an area where it was safe to come to a crouch and then work your way to the rear. It was important for men always in action to get some time to think without fear, more or less. They needed to give the eyes and the mind a chance to rest. That meant getting back to our HQ unit – platoon or company headquarters – where some respite from machine-gun and mortar fire could be found.

Gaimanche

Hot Water and Clean Underwear
July 12 to July 18, 1944

On July 12, the battalion was withdrawn to a rest station called Gaimanche. The week gave us a chance to clean up, put on some clean clothes and discuss what had happened, the mistakes that might have been made, how we could correct them in the future and so on. We had been very fortunate. Even though we had lost many officers and NCOs, others would step forward from the ranks taking over the job of leadership. The men were so well trained that every soldier could lead a platoon if necessary. The training we had received over the last four years was priceless.

In the rest area we also got the chance to write some real letters home. In general, most soldiers sent a letter as often as possible, but usually just a small card. In battle conditions, after they had dug in, arranged camouflage and put out their flares, each would almost automatically take out a pencil (pens couldn't stand up to the rough life) and get off a short note on one of these cards. But at a rest area they could do better.

Rest stations like Gaimanche, however, were not entirely tourist areas. We were still under artillery fire. The fire at times was heavy and very well planned. At least enemy aircraft were not a problem for us ground troops. There was some ambush bombing on a few nights – two or three planes trying a sneak attack – but generally the Luftwaffe had taken off for other territory.

Gaimanche was also the scene of an incident that others probably are still laughing about. But I was pretty upset at the time. Here's a "stripped down" version from my viewpoint.

At Gaimanche they had a mobile bath set-up so you could get what they called a shower. Everybody got water, and if you were lucky, you got hot water. Most of us thought there weren't really any heaters despite the advertising. At any rate, it was mostly cold water for us. Each soldier was given clean socks and underwear. In my case a little problem arose. After I had stripped and run through the mobile bath, the quartermaster managing the thing said, "Well, seeing that you had no underwear coming in, you cannot have any replacement underwear."

Now, we had worn one set of underwear since May – back at some place in England – and we hadn't had any chance to really wash it. We could rinse it out sometimes and try hanging it in the slit trench to dry. That really wasn't a good particularly good idea. So I had thrown mine away. There followed with the quartermaster and me what you might call a slight disagreement. I picked up a Bren gun and went after him, yelling and shouting. Stark naked, waving the Bren and hollering like mad, I chased him through the village.

There was no magazine in the Bren. But he didn't know that.

When I went back to the mobile bath, there was no trouble getting my new underwear. It had suddenly become so quiet, in fact, that I helped myself to a spare set.

The Queen's Own Rifles held the position at Gaimanche for the next eight days. In this holding period at our rest station, we lost over thirty soldiers killed or wounded from enemy fire that was ever present.

Battles of Colombelles and Giberville

An Objective Too Far
July 18, 1944

After Caen and Carpiquet, the following battles at Colombelles and Giberville should have been one single action. But the start line was not wholly under Allied control. The Canadians, therefore, were first given the task of capturing Colombelles – a northerly industrial suburb of Caen dominated by tall factory chimneys and similar structures offering the enemy good observation opportunities. It turned out that the enemy troops were strongly entrenched in the factory area, which was not the briefing information we'd been given.

The action started on July 18 at 7:00 a.m. with A and B companies. We took a lot of prisoners. A cruel and inexplicable act was committed by a prisoner who had been wounded. One of our QOR stretcher-bearers bandaged up his leg, and when we started moving forward again, the man pulled his pistol and began firing into the backs of those who had helped him. He killed one of our men, a man who had already been wounded.

In the turmoil, as we grabbed his weapon away from him, his arm was broken and he was pretty roughed up. A group of prisoners carried him back on a four-by-eight-foot sheet of corrugated iron with a note attached for the military police explaining what he'd done. But we never heard anything further. I suppose he might have been an officer from the Russian front who assumed he was being sent off for execution.

This was to be another sad day of losses for A Company and for the men from June 1940. Giberville was ultimately taken, the objective we'd been given at the briefing, but the loss of three new platoon leaders and then the veteran Buck Hawkins was painful

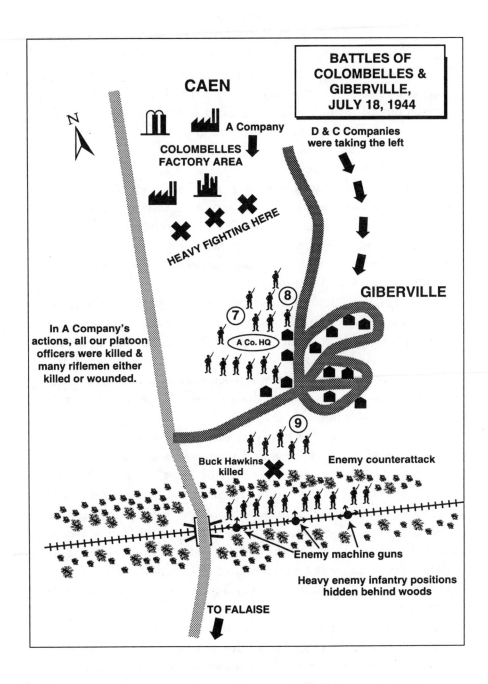

CAEN

BATTLES OF
COLOMBELLES &
GIBERVILLE,
JULY 18, 1944

A Company

COLOMBELLES
FACTORY AREA

D & C Companies
were taking the left

HEAVY FIGHTING HERE

GIBERVILLE

In A Company's
actions, all our platoon
officers were killed &
many riflemen either
killed or wounded.

⑦

⑧

A Co. HQ

⑨

Buck Hawkins
killed

Enemy counterattack

Enemy machine guns

Heavy enemy infantry positions
hidden behind woods

TO FALAISE

and tragic for us all. Buck was taken from us almost at the last minute. Had his section dug in and stayed at the objective, things might have been alright. But it did not work out that way.

Giberville is a typical tiny French village, a group of buildings and houses facing each other in the centre of town. The farms stretch out all around, something like a wheel, and the hub is the village itself. By this time in July the grain was nearly ready for the harvest. The heads were almost formed, and other fields around Giberville were in hay or turnips.

Heavy crossfire was coming from the village. A Company achieved the objective, but in the action we lost all of our newly arrived platoon commanders – Gerry Rayner, Jim McNeeley and Ken MacLeod. All three had been with us earlier. They'd been promoted from the ranks and had just been sent back to us from OCTU (Officer Cadet Training Unit).

George Bennett took five machine-gun bullets in the stomach; Gérard Brière and Bert Shepherd were also wounded that day. We managed to set up a first-aid post in the village, but the continuing crossfire made it impossible to take out the wounded. Among our many prisoners was a sergeant who had some medical training, and he organized some sort of operating room in one of the bigger houses.

After the loss of our new platoon leaders, Cpl. Jack Bennett and "the Kid" took over 8 and 9 platoons. Both were corporals, but the second was always known by his nickname. He was Jackie Bland and his platoon included the very special Buck Hawkins. For some reason – possibly the briefing instructions about the objective given to the new lieutenants had not been passed on properly to all the NCOs – parts of both platoons on their own initiative left our objective at Giberville. They moved forward to a hedgerow and railway line about four hundred yards farther south.

The road with its hedgerow and rail junction must have looked like an easy place to capture and hold. There were good views to the south and north. It probably appeared to be an easy takeover. Appearances, however, can be deceiving. This old saying was proven again as the enemy suddenly came out of the woods and through a heavy hedge that had screened them. They counterattacked with about two companies – there were three to four hundred men – line abreast and coming straight on.

While the others gave me covering fire, I made my way forward to tell them a barrage was about to come in and that they'd better drop back to the village before the mortar fire started. At the same time I sent Charlie Bloomfield to Company HQ with a message calling for smoke, artillery and mortars to land directly on this forward position. Most of both platoons up there managed to pull back okay to the village, partly because Buck insisted on staying put to give covering fire. Jackie Bland said he'd stay with Buck, and both Jimmy Young and Steve de Blois said the same. They stayed till no ammunition was left.

Then, as our small remnant started to pull back before our barrage came in, Buck was hit by a full blast of enemy machine-gun fire, probably in one of the sweeps supporting their advance.

Later that day, though fire was still coming in, we went back for Buck and brought him in. We were in tears about our comrade and the fluke MG fire that had taken him. Buck's loss also painfully brought home to us that three out of four of the D-Day men from our three platoons had now gone.

Four of the D-Day soldiers – Jackie Bland, Jeff Oliver, Ernie Hackett and myself – carried him back on a barn door to the village church. He had stayed with his Bren while holding back over three hundred of the enemy. He had known very well how perilously vulnerable we were. Our fighting strength was just six men to a section, instead of ten or twelve, and only eighteen to twenty men to a platoon – 50 percent of what it should have been. Buck was the type to try to make up for it all by himself.

Harry Henry Hawkins was considerably older than most of us, or so it seemed at the time. Consequently, in England they had sensibly posted Buck as a corporal. The night he was given the promotion, he went out with the crowd. Most were younger men in their very early twenties or less; he was old enough to be their father. Next morning when he was called for parade, he said to me, "Please ask the Major to take back those stripes. I can't ask these boys to give up their lives for me."

Buck Hawkins at thirty-nine was fourteen years up on me. He'd always been a close companion. He had been born in England and had come to Canada as a youngster, pretty much in the same way I had. He left a wife and two daughters – Helen and Annabelle – at home in Toronto. He was six two, 190 pounds, kind and brave, a natural leader, fearless in action. He was offered stripes again many times, but always refused them. Buck had a natural sense in combat. Many were the times we had all put faith in that intuition and turned to him to say, "What do you think, Buck?" No words could express our feelings for Buck. The pain that day cannot be described.

We stayed at Giberville, consolidating our position, till July 21. During this time – and in fact throughout the campaign – the cooperation of the support units was above the normal line of duty. This was very important for the morale of the men, especially getting a hot meal at least once a day. Otherwise we simply would have had to survive on rations we called "compo," tasteless and cold packages of so-called stews and other products of uncertain origin.

For a brief time at the beginning of our action at Giberville, we faced a situation that demanded we be somewhat resourceful. We had no food of any great account except what we could pack in the carrier, and that was full of Brens, ammo and shovels. So in the village the ever-resourceful Canadians, scrounging from the countryside, discovered an enormous cast-iron cooking pot. Into this makeshift super-cooker we tossed all the odds and ends we could find around the village. Turnips were plentiful, and I think we even threw in some tulip bulbs as well. Over the next two or three days, until the British tanks came in from the left flank, we actually fed the whole company from this soup pot. This was an example once again of the Canadian soldier's skill at making things work as the need arose.

A Company and its three platoons were specially resourceful. I've already mentioned the platoons' nicknames, but they bear repeating here. 7 Platoon were mostly from Geraldton, so they were the Miners. 8 Platoon was from the heart of old downtown Toronto, some pretty tough neighbourhoods, so they were the Cabbagetowners. My old 9 Platoon, drawn mostly from Toronto West, were dubbed the Farmers. This all provided some great rivalry, maybe in the beginning a bit overdone, but in tough training mean spirits do not last long, and in combat that's doubly so. And we came to appreciate one another's specialties.

Our men in these three platoons surpassed all others in adaptability. They could adjust to anything. For example, it was not too long after D-Day before we had our company carrier stuffed with all we'd need in unusual circumstances – five extra Brens and lots of ammunition, four gallons of rum, spare shovels, axes, picks, cigarettes, bandages, candles and fuel for cooking fires.

Some of this resourcefulness may have had some uncertain roots. Back in our Newfoundland training days we had to dig trenches in ground that looked and felt like sheer rock. Picks weren't making a dent. We looked around for an alternative. As it happened, the Americans were there building the airport at Gander. They had all kinds of material in rows of storage sheds. A few of us liberated a box of their dynamite, sort of our own lend/lease program. They were paid so much more than we were that it seemed we were only drawing a small credit.

I had my farm experience to go by, having used the stuff to clear stumps or blow up rocks. That night, to create a few easy foxholes for us, I used a little too much. There were too many helpers, and each seemed to be saying, "Hey Charlie, put in another coupla sticks – do it right." With all this enthusiasm from those who were fed up with their digging, the explosion ended up being so enormous that every light on the base came on. They thought they were being shelled by the ghost of the *Graf Spee,* a famous pocket-battleship that had been scuttled a year or so earlier.

We were all paraded the next day. Nobody said a word.

Grentheville, Bourquébus Ridge and Fontaine Henry

Beaches – This Time Friendly
July 21 to August 8, 1944

After Giberville and its consolidation, we were ordered on July 21 to Grentheville, a village a few miles away, where we stayed till midnight July 26. The day before we left, something happened that stays with me yet. Lindy Lindenas and I were sharing a slit trench. We were in a holding position while the enemy kept us under steady fire – 88s, mortars and Moaning Minnies. Lindy had gone over to company headquarters and I was about ready to go for my regular check on the hot meal that the men had every day.

Along came our company stretcher-bearer* up from Battalion HQ. He was a very kind, gentle person and I guess maybe he'd had a lot to do that day. He said he was so tired out, didn't know where to go under all the constant fire, so I said, "Well sure, use our slit trench – Lindy's gone and I've other things to do." He was glad to stretch out. I had not gone farther than ten feet when an 88 shell landed right in our trench. He was killed instantly. The blast knocked me for quite a few yards.

I always felt so upset whenever anyone was hurt or killed – I'm still that way – and that particular incident is hard for me to forget.

By dawn of July 27, we were in position on Bourquébus Ridge, a key area for the approaching action at Falaise. We left the ridge on July 31 to move back to Fontaine Henry, eight miles

---

* Rfn. S.E. Armitage.

from the front line, for a week's rest. We were safely out of
artillery range for the first time since D-Day. For fifty-six consec-
utive days the action had been heavy, almost constant, always terrifying, and every man in the Queen's Own had performed
beyond words – much more than duty demanded.

The week's rest we had at Fontaine Henry was the first time
in sixty days that our soldiers could have ten to twelve hours
sleep. Every man needed it. We even went to the beach. And this
one was almost like those at home. It was a bit strange to discover
at last that beaches in Europe could also be friendly.

We had some shows, repaired equipment, cleaned guns and
best of all had "regular" meals. The battalion cooks were good to
us. You can imagine that after about two months of Normandy
action, there were no complaints about the three hot meals a
day.

During this time, one of our originals and one of our best in
the silent patrols, Wilf Mercer, left us. There were new flame-
throwing carriers called Wasps available to our forces, and Wilf
became a sergeant with one of them. He had been with us on D-
Day; when we had moved through the village of Bernières-sur-
Mer he had taken the left side of the church. He was a great guy
with any kind of machinery, so I suppose the idea of these huge
flame throwers, which had to be towed by a Bren carrier, did not
frighten him as much as they would some of the rest of us.

They took only volunteers, because you were in reality offering yourself as a captive inside a vulnerable and deadly target.
With the portable manpacks you were also a target, but at least
you could dump them in a hurry.

Near the end of the war as we moved forward to the Rhine,
we were in a very tough action and Wilf lost his leg. He was
trapped inside and yelling for us to get away before the thrower
blew up. Some of his old-timer friends from the section helped to
get him out just in the nick of time; we'll come to that later.

With such transfers, preparations and other breaks from the
action of the previous two months, we made ready for Falaise.

Quesnay Wood on the Road to Falaise

Hedgerow by Hedgerow
August 9, 10 and 11, 1944

This battle was yet another phase after the Caen break-out and our ultimate push to Falaise itself, where we intended to meet the American forces and thus "close the gap" and encircle the enemy. Maj. Steve Lett had briefed the company commanders about Quesnay Wood, twenty acres of bush about two miles ahead of us down a country road, which at this point had farm fields and orchards going back around eight hundred yards on each side. There wasn't a whole lot of information about the task. For some reason we did not go straight ahead down the road itself, which would have been my choice. We were given the fields on each side of the road. A Company took the farm fields on the right side of the road, and B Company took those on the left. The other two companies stood by, ready to be committed if required.

Country roads in France are often about the same as those in England. And the Falaise Road was typical. Though it looked large enough to us at the time, it was just an ordinary road, only wide enough to allow two wagons to pass, low in the centre, and with hedgerows along each side. In Quesnay Wood, which was about seven miles north of Falaise, there was bush on both sides of the road but heavier on the left. Assorted grain fields and orchards surrounded or preceded the woods in a patchwork quilt arrangement.

There has always been some difference of opinion as to the start time, but my recollection is that although we'd been ready since dawn, we weren't given the order until after eleven o'clock, or even closer to noon. There'd been a delay because the battalion commander had been waiting for the Polish tanks to join us. We didn't know it, but they'd been caught in the accidental bombing of our forces at Caen and for some reason the report of their loss had not been passed forward. Finally we quit waiting and moved out.

The battle was preceded by a time of great quiet. Silence seemed to lie over the whole area. I'm not certain that we knew at the time just how significant our assignment was and how much was expected of it. There's no doubt the support of the Polish tanks would have made an enormous difference to us. We had some artillery support, but one look at those woods ahead foretold how difficult finding a target would be.

The idea was that B Company on the left and ourselves on the right should advance, capture a strong point and then have the two remaining companies move through us and take the high ground a few miles farther. This would put them in a position overlooking Falaise. In retrospect, the plan seems, well, ambitious.

We covered about a mile and a bit and stopped around eight hundred yards from the woods. We knew they were in there – you could see the activity, although the targets were well hidden by the heavy trees and bush. Each company, left of the road and right of the road, had a real challenge. Both areas were divided into fields, marked by typical hedgerows of stone and dirt two to three feet high, with growth on top of that of another seven feet or so. These contained plenty of enemy positions that had to be cleared out one by one. Then, in every other field or so, there'd be a double hedgerow with a sunken lane between. Once these lanes were cleared and made secure, our carrier used them to bring up more ammo, which we were going through at a tremendous rate.

Because the hedgerows offered such good defence to the enemy, our Bren-gunners were pouring it on, covering the riflemen as they advanced. Often we'd be right on the enemy position before the defenders – pinned down by the Bren fire – realized it. Then they'd give up rather easily, surprised to be overrun. In their defence, it should be said they had a poor field of fire in those hedgerows; as long as our ammo held out we could pin them down and pretty well get right up to them. We usually told the survivors to discard their weapons, put their hands on their heads and move back to our lines.

In this way on our side of the road, we slowly moved up, field by field, hedgerow by hedgerow, using our Brens and some mortars with good effect. We had no way of knowing how the other company on the left of the road was proceeding, though we could hear the fire.

By late afternoon we'd covered maybe six hundred yards, or three-quarters of the distance to the woods. We were troops fairly well battlewise at this point and did not get too upset about the troubles we'd gone through to get this far. We had some wounded, and the continuing need for ammunition supplies was always a concern.

About this time, 9 Platoon made a move and got up to the last hedgerow before the woods. We knew by now that the woods contained dug-in 88s and heavy machine guns. In fact, they had us targeted very well. About 250 yards from the woods and 100 feet from the road was exactly where 80 percent of their fire was landing.

I had spent the afternoon moving from section to section, back to HQ and Boss Medland, then forward again with new instructions, and always checking to make sure the carrier was available with the ammunition supply.*

So when I got up to 9 Platoon, there was some decision to be made. Should we dig in? Should we wait for the tanks? By this time several runners had gone back as each new piece of information was obtained. But we had no way of knowing, either at our forward point or back at A Company HQ, that on the other side of the road B Company had run into real trouble. One section under Lieut. J.F. Lake had managed to get into the woods, but the fire

---

* In this type of action, Charlie carried no weapon except his pistol ("if I needed a rifle I could always pick one up from one of the wounded") and wore no helmet, preferring his camouflage net which he wore as a kind of veiled shroud over his head and shoulders. He had his fully loaded Smith & Wesson and six extra rounds; during the course of this action, he used nine.

they took was killing, probably more than we were taking. At any rate, his section was shot up, and he was wounded in both legs. The unit in reserve (C Company) had already been committed on that side, and all in all they were having it pretty tough. But all we knew on our side is that we had our own share of dug-in 88s and heavy machine guns facing us, and the intensity of the fire was incredible, about as bad as we had taken back at Carpiquet.

I moved from the centre of the attack over to the left and hooked up with Jimmy Sackfield, Sid Willis, Percy McNab, Ernie Hackett, Jack Morgan and Charlie Bloomfield. We knew we couldn't stay put. Not only could the enemy drop their fire right on us, but we were also committed to keep moving forward, since we were expecting D Company to come up and move through us. It was essential to keep moving; this was our training.

Even if we'd known of the serious difficulty B and C were in, it probably wouldn't have changed anything for us. We started off, about seven to ten feet apart. Jimmy Sackfield and Sid Willis were our point men. We got about fifty feet when they opened up. Sid died instantly. Jimmy took a machine-gun bullet in the right shoulder; it hit the blade of his shovel (on his back pack) and bounced out the left shoulder. Nonetheless we thought he'd probably be okay. They took him back to the hedgerow and called for a stretcher. We learned later that he died the next day.

Farther to the left we were luckier. After laying down a heavy cover of smoke and mortars, we got to within sixty feet or so of the woods. We had come to the "finish" of the field, where the wheat is no longer waist high but scraggly and sparse, and the land drops off a little to a drainage area. Here the farmer plows in such a way that the good soil is pushed out to higher ground and sunlight, away from the shade of the hedgerow. Without the cover the wheat had provided, we were lucky to find a small fur-row. We crept along it – very slow, very quiet – right up to the hedgerow at the edge of the woods. Good luck again – there was a drainage ditch going from the field into the woods and we were glad to follow it.

So we're there. Once again we faced the question, now what?

First of all we spotted three heavies dug in at the edge of the woods and firing out. Being up close to a tank is not so bad; they can't see what's under them, only what's fairly far in front. We were in sort of a low area, swampy in the spring but dry now, with small shrubs around – a good hiding place. We sent Charlie Bloomfield and Ernie Hackett back with all the information we could assemble – number of tanks, location, estimate of the number of troops, etc. – with a request for ammunition, and a Piat gun that would help us (not by much – that armour plate was too much) against the tanks. We were prepared to hold on, depending on HQ instructions and whatever tank, artillery or air support they might plan. Otherwise, we said, we'd pull out around midnight, when things generally seem to quiet down, and get back to HQ about dawn.

How Charlie and Ernie made it back to HQ was a miracle. Not only that, but Charlie returned to us with a message and precious ammunition. He told us the action had been stopped that afternoon and that we should bring everyone back to the starting area before our barrage came in.

We'd been sitting there dead quiet all that time with empty weapons. All we'd had among us were the last three rounds in my .38 and we were watching the enemy very, very carefully. By that time, 8 Platoon had also got the message and had started back. So we all returned to our HQ position, organized our defence and began to count our losses.

It was still dark, the dawn perhaps another hour or so away. Padre J. Stewart asked for volunteers and some of us went out to check the hedgerows and wheat fields for the wounded. These were taken out. We had to be very quiet; at night noise carries farther. When we found a man he'd get a shot of morphine immediately. This was for the pain, but also to ensure his silence. They were still laying down mortars, artillery and machine guns at the slightest sound, and of course by that time they were super-nervous about another attack.

In combat everything is magnified. Quesnay Wood is only twenty acres or so but it could just as well have been Algonquin

Park. The full weight of the remaining enemy armour was concentrated at this area to protect the Falaise Road, which they had to keep open as long as possible. Our support had great difficulty pinpointing the site of each tank. The enemy probably had chosen wisely. Good, solid, mature trees in the bush gave them cover from bombing or artillery fire. The thick and heavy underbrush we encountered made our ground movement difficult. And the enemy proved to be very, very skilled.

Quesnay Wood was a battle, not really of errors, but certainly of unfortunate events. The expected Polish division of tanks, which was to have supported us in the attack, had been misidentified and caught in heavy bombing by the Americans. Our battalion commander, not knowing the tanks had been knocked out of action, had continued to expect support that had no chance of arriving. Because the enemy tanks were well protected by the woods, our artillery had trouble pinpointing them. For example, when C Company asked for artillery support, it was delivered too far in advance of the men to be of much value in their assault.

And it's a bit of a mystery to me why we didn't use the road. That option might have been more productive than hedgerow by hedgerow.

In this battle, which was successful only in that we took our own start point, the Queen's Own lost eighty-five men. The biggest number of casualties were in B and C companies. Nonetheless, although no ground had been gained, yet another concentrated force had been pretty well broken up.

After that long day and long night, there was another tragic loss. As we moved forward the following day, a sniper's bullet found its way to Jimmy Browne.

Jimmy Browne had been one of the original miners who came from Geraldton and the Long Lac area. They had left their jobs in the mines and with two first war veterans leading the way (Sergeant Conrad and Mr. Wilson), the whole group had come to join the regiment in Toronto.

Gentle, steady and thoroughly reliable, Jimmy quickly became 7 Platoon's top NCO. In fact, for 80 percent of the time in

Normandy he was really the platoon leader. When Elliot Dalton, our company commander, was wounded at Le Mesnil-Patry, their platoon leader (Jack Pond) moved up to take over from Elliot. Jimmy then filled in as 7's platoon leader. Replacements eventually came, which included a new lieutenant. But in our costly action at Colombelles, that officer was lost in his first battle. Jimmy quickly and reliably took over once again.

Jimmy Browne was about five ten and 185 pounds. He was one of those people who never seemed to raise their voice. Had I been the company commander in England when the call came for a CSM, my choice would have been Jimmy. The Miners had many good men. I had already chosen their senior corporal (Charlie Smith) to take over my old job as sergeant of 9 Platoon. Both Jimmy and Charlie were so well liked and so capable that I had expected problems in my new job as company sergeant-major. But that was never the case. They gave me all the cooperation possible.

Though Jimmy had worked in the Geraldton mines, he was from Winnipeg. He used to send regular letters to his father, who still lived there. And letters to a beautiful girl in Hamilton. She had come to visit him at Camp Borden before our posting to Newfoundland. A few days before the Quesnay Wood attack, Jimmy gave me two letters – one for Winnipeg and one for Hamilton – saying if anything happened to him, to please mail these. He'd never done or said anything like that before. It was strange.

After the war I visited his father in Winnipeg. I tried to get round to all of the parents or wives of those who had been lost. A curious thing about such visits was that the wives were pretty good about the stiff upper lip treatment; once in a while they could be even more remote than that. But the parents were another matter. That's the way it was in Winnipeg with Jimmy's father. It was a tough visit.

In any case, Jimmy was well loved, and not least by the men of 7 Platoon. When he was killed by a sniper's bullet, sadness filled the air like lead. His loss was mourned for a long time after.

Robert-Mesnil and Maizières on the Falaise Road

August 11 to August 17, 1944

After Quesnay Wood, we were able to move forward another mile or two closer to Falaise. Now the push began from the village of Robert-Mesnil with an attack August 14 on the village of Maizières. The men were loaded in Kangaroos (armoured personnel carriers). When the carriers moved forward to attack, twenty-four men were killed or wounded.

This day too saw a serious mistake on the part of the air forces of the Allies in their attempt at support our attack. We learned painfully that in the absence of ground-to-air communication, positions and troops can easily be misidentified.

Our attack this day was to involve the tactical support of both Bomber Command's Lancasters and the American B17s (Flying Fortresses) from the U.S. Army Air Force. Air cover to this point had generally been far in advance, which was absolutely necessary to soften up the objectives. This day, however, was intended to be "close support." The final signal for us came about noon. All was quiet; we were moving forward. Suddenly from out of nowhere bombs were landing on our own forces from American bombers flying at high altitude (we couldn't see them). Pretty scary, mildly speaking.

Then about three hours later, the Lancasters flew over at about a hundred yards. We could see the pilots at the controls, bomb doors opening and the bombs dropping. Talk about fear! We were helpless. Other British planes, who seemed to know better, were swarming their own bombers, shooting and stunting, trying to warn them away. Yellow smoke was everywhere. It was our only possible signal to identify ourselves as friendly. We pumped out so much of it you'd choke. Unfortunately, its value was uncertain because the enemy had learned to protect themselves using the same stunt.*

To finish the day, a few Luftwaffe planes got in that night to drop bombs on our positions.

This third bombing was another example of my luck. I was making my regular rounds that evening. Everyone had had his hot meal, we were safely dug in, and things seemed quiet. I started digging my own slit trench and then thought, heck, look at that lovely large house that's entirely empty. I helped myself to one of the nicer bedrooms and made a pillow with my cocked pistol under it. I always slept that way, especially after seeing Tommy's section shot at Le Mesnil-Patry; nobody was going to take me prisoner. Then an enormous bang! The entire world seemed to shake. I went out to look and saw my partial slit trench had now become a hole eight feet deep – a direct hit by a bomb, probably a 500-pounder.

---

* Top secret documents describing "Bombing Errors in Close Support Operation of August 14, 1944" were classified until June 12, 1972. They reveal a massive inquiry headed by Bomber Harris (Air Chief Marshall Arthur T. Harris) with footnotes in his handwriting. From the papers these selected notes are offered to explain the inexplicable: " ... proposal involved a heavy bomber attack on enemy concentrations which formed a deep salient in the Army lines, and obviously involved serious risk to our troops ... 800 aircraft were dispatched against seven enemy concentrations all within 2000 yards of the Canadians striking towards Falaise ... The following errors occurred during the bombing ... 14 a/c bombed St. Aigran (twice), 23 a/c bombed Haut Mesnil Quarry, 26 a/c bombed Haut Mesnil Quarry ... total of 77 aircraft mistook the aiming point (27 a/c 1 Group, 4 a/c 4 Group, 44 a/c 6 Group, 2 a/c 8 Group Pathfinder Force) ..."

After the inquiry, Arthur Harris listed in his report eleven causal conditions emphasizing "the over-ready relinquishment of the timed run check from the coastline by the Captains and Navigators implicated."

The two Pathfinder Force crews were ordered to turn in their badges and acting ranks "consequent upon Pathfinder employ" and were re-posted to ordinary crew duties. Squadron and flight commanders implicated received the same treatment. All crews implicated were "starred" – not to be within thirty miles forward of the bomb line.

The formations mentioned "suffering from the bombardment" were 2nd Canadian AGRA – HQ; 1st Polish Armoured Division; HQ of Brigades of the 3rd Canadian Infantry Division and some units of the 4th Canadian Infantry Brigade.

Later when others viewed this example of my great good fortune, there was some restraint in their reaction. Some grumblers in the outfit even seemed resentful that I had reconnoitred such a nice bedroom for myself. One sceptic was heard to say, "Yeah – where's the blonde?" Happily, Vi was doing her job at the guns back in England and didn't hear the gripes of these malcontents who had spent their night in the ground.

Well, blondes or not, that was sheer good luck, clearly. Maybe that's why some idea seemed to develop that luck followed me around. For example, earlier that day we had a chap sitting on the side of the jeep bathing his feet. It was important to keep your feet in good condition. Then the bombs came and he took off like a deer. We didn't see him for about five hours and had begun to think something had gone wrong when he turned up riding a carrier. His bare feet had become an awful bloody mess. He said he was so scared he'd run back practically to the beach. We bandaged his feet and asked him to go to First Aid. "No bloody way," he said, "from now on I'm staying as close to you as I can." He seemed to think that I was in charge of the luck department.

NOTE: *Charlie Martin doesn't include the good luck story of all time in these recollections. To him, it's a Buck Hawkins story. But it belongs with luck stories and here's why:*

Back in Sussex, New Brunswick, embarkation for England was due. Charlie and Buck had a five-day leave. There were two problems in this. One was the train travel; it took two days to get to Toronto and two days to get back. This left them with only one short day. Due to leave for England and all that lay before them, this was especially hard for Buck, who always missed his wife and their two daughters; he talked about them all the time. The other was money; a return ticket was $28.

One of those affairs was coming up where footraces, a tug of war and other events would pit team against team. The purpose was to build morale, keep the boys fit and that sort of thing. If some in A

Company could do well, said the Major, there'd be an extra three-day pass. Charlie and Buck got themselves on various teams. Charlie was a fast runner; Buck was good on the rope. One way or another, they qualified for the pass. The net value of the extra pass would be four days at home instead of one. First problem half solved.

Second problem. For some reason at month end, they'd not been paid. Charlie had $1.25 in his pocket; Buck had 75 cents. Great happiness, however, prevailed with the adjacent Chaudières, who had not only been paid but were having a gigantic crap game. The two wandered over and when their turn at the dice came, Buck said to Charlie, "You take the dice and let's see what you can do."

"How much should we put in?" Charlie asked.

"All of it," was the quiet answer.

So while the Chaudières yelled to get on with the game, they gingerly put forward their tiny handful of change amounting to about two dollars, which was immediately covered.

Charlie rolled a seven.

"Let it ride," said Buck quietly.

The other players easily covered the four dollars, and on this second roll-out, the Chaudières could see an easy victory looming for the eight dollars in the pot.

Out came eleven. The players roared; they were going to need to work harder to recover their investment. And most sensible shooters would drag some of the pot at this point, delaying the recovery even more.

"Let it ride," said Buck quietly, carefully eyeing the money coming in to cover their eight dollars, making sure everybody was in and a full sixteen dollars in the pot.

This time, as best Charlie can recall, there was a point to be made and as the yelling rose, sure enough out came the point. They'd built up the pot by a lot – two dollars of theirs and fourteen from the game.

"Let it ride," said Buck, still quietly.

The Chaudières could smell blood now. They rushed and elbowed their way to grab this easy money. So many passes in a row were unusual; the shooter was overdue for a crapout. They fought to *get their money down — easy pickings and the crowd was roaring. Sixteen dollars covered now, and the shooter coming out for a $32 pot.*

Seven.

The roof of the Quonset almost came off. The losers cursed this apple-picking farm boy. Surely now any shooter would claim a pay-day, drag his profit and go back to his original stake. The rage at this injustice filled the room.

"What now, Buck?" Charlie asked. He was almost at Buck's ear for this urgent counsel; the din in the hut was deafening.

"Let it ride," said Buck, maybe not quite so quietly this time.

New players had come forward. Only a few had hung in for the trip. Now the pot was serious. Most of the players were looking at close to a month's pay sitting there, up for grabs. Little piles were divided up as the shouts went up — "I've got two" — "Mine's five dollars" — "Gimme ten bucks and a snake eyes" — and Buck eyeballed how the $32 was covered. Charlie looked at the dice in his hand, shook them once and rolled for the fifth time.

Seven. And a $64 pot, up from two bucks.

Immediately a hand the size of a baseball glove appeared. In a second Buck had scooped up the money. "That's enough, Charlie," he said and made for the door. Charlie was right behind him.

Nobody could describe the rage of the Chaudières. There was pandemonium and eventually a riot. The report was in the newspaper the next day.

Now they had their $56 for the train tickets and a little to spare. But they still needed the extra three-day pass. Time was short; they needed to hustle.

Charlie went to the orderly room. Were the passes ready? "No," said the corporal at the desk, "but the requisitions are here all made out. You just have to get the Major to sign them. And he's gone to the toilet."

Charlie took the requisitions and made for the washroom. The man was still buttoning his pants when Charlie came in.

"Sir, could you please sign these requisitions for our passes?"

Predictably, the Major huffed.

"I could have you on charge for barging in here like this." It was almost a grunt.

"But sir, you promised, and I am being respectful," Charlie countered in his best tone.

When Charlie came out of the washroom, he had the signed requisitions in his hand. He and Buck made for the railway station, carefully avoiding any rampaging Chaudières or the MPs.

Charlie tells this story under the heading of Buck's last leave. He just remembers it as how they got Buck four days at home with the family before leaving Canada.

It seems the Major was something of a pukka type while he was stationed in Canada; wouldn't normally speak to an enlisted man, crusty and aloof. Charlie saw him again in an action near the end of the war. He'll appear later.

Maizières

Scenes of Total War
August 17 to August 23, 1944

It was late in the afternoon when we finally occupied Maizières. The capture of Falaise itself took place later by other forces that advanced through us. Falaise, Maizières and all the small centres in the entire area had become pretty much a slaughter house for the enemy forces. We had plenty of work assembling prisoners, clearing out resistance pockets and always probing with our patrols.

It was not pretty. The roads leading out of Maizières, Grand-Mesnil and other villages were strewn with burnt or abandoned tanks, trucks, wagons, artillery, and dead horses.

Throughout the Normandy battles, burnt-out tanks, trucks and homes had often filled the countryside with an odour we found hard to stomach. But this was worse. The sunken roads – almost wagon tracks really, with hedgerows along each side – were littered every foot of the way with corpses and burned equipment. The stench made us sick. This was an awful price of war – the bodies of enemy soldiers, dead horses and cows, broken wagons, disabled anti-tank guns and burned trucks. All of this had to be cleared before any movement on these roads would be possible.

Tragically there were many civilians – mothers, children and families – all innocent victims of this carnage. In the heat of August, it did not take long for the bloating to start. The stench was everywhere. The enemy in its rush to get out had left both the dead and the wounded where they fell, grotesque and stinking reminders of what war can cause.

These enemy corpses were probably not the same forces who just four years ago, in their boastful occupation of this country and of practically all Europe, had bombed and strafed civilians, innocents who had choked the escape roads with handcarts and baby carriages, only to be machine-gunned so that these routes could be cleared for military vehicles. There seemed no explanation for all this cruelty, destruction and stench. We had all come to France, every soldier in the QOR and throughout the army, knowing there was a job to be done. We had done that job. The cost had been hard for us, but at Falaise the collapse of the enemy forces and the devastation they had brought on themselves and on others seemed an awful testimony to a regime that lasted not a thousand years, but barely twelve.

Through all of this terrible aftermath of battle, French civilians were recovering the bodies of their own loved ones. The French were friendly and kind to us, but the tears were there and sometimes it was clear they had to try very hard to smile and wave a welcome at their Canadian liberators. We were welcomed warmly, there's no doubt on that score. But many families had private grief, although they did their best to hide it from us.

We had come to learn the full meaning of total war. Violence begets violence. In this war, in just over two months, we had already seen too much of it, learning in the cruelest way that to survive, and to carry the day, meant total war and all that came with it.

We were not long at Maizières. About August 20 we moved ten miles east of Falaise to Grand-Mesnil. Despite the ring we helped to close at Falaise and the destruction of countless enemy divisions and special formations, there was much yet ahead of us. The Channel ports were still enemy occupied; parts of France had yet to be consolidated; and the Rhineland and Northern Holland were still ahead for the QORs.

The capture of Falaise was the end of our Normandy action. Some say it should also have marked the end of the war. But the enemy refused to recognize a defeat that now was inevitable. Hitler's folly, I call it.

The consequence of holding out until after we on the west had crossed the Rhine and the Russians on the east had advanced to Berlin was without any benefit at all to the enemy forces or to their nation. The long eight months ahead simply meant more loss of life for everyone.

Unaware of these considerations at the time, we prepared to get on with the job and advance to our next assignment. We had finished seventy-eight days of action that took us from our D-Day landing at Bernières-sur-Mer to the battle for Falaise. We had lost three-quarters of our original force; so many of our best friends and finest fighters had been taken. Less than one out of four of us remained. Our reinforcements had paid an almost equal cost: 50 percent dead or wounded in that time.

These seventy-eight days had seen great challenges and painful losses for the Queen's Own.

After Normandy

The Changes Sink In

The battle of Normandy was over. The enemy fought hard, but their consequence was ruin. Their SS divisions were mangled and needed massive reinforcement.

Now as we started to advance across France, several things came to mind. We had been so very busy and under such tremendous stress, each success so very hard won, but we felt satisfied with the job. We were all pleased with the record of A Company; all the wounded had been picked up right away and all our objectives captured and held. We were fortunate, but now we had a very different A Company from those 120 or so who had landed on the beaches June 6. Not too many of us originals were left.

We now had three new platoon commanders and three new sergeants. Lieut. A.E. King and Joe Meagher, on D-Day a rifleman but now a sergeant, headed up 7 Platoon. Lieut. Jack Boos and Bill Lennox, a corporal on D-Day and now a sergeant, had 8 Platoon. And 9 Platoon now had Lieut. Gordon Haynes* and "the Kid," Jackie Bland, who was another D-Day rifleman who had moved up to sergeant.

Bill Bettridge and Jim McCullough were transferred to a scout platoon, newly formed. This new unit drew some of the best men for advance work in situations that would make good use of their experience in patrols.

Bill Ross, who had been wounded earlier in Normandy, joined Jack Martin in our mortar platoon. It seemed whenever

---

* Gordon Haynes, promoted from the ranks, stayed in after the war and went on to become a full colonel.

A Company asked for supporting mortar fire, we could always count on them. A great deal of credit for the capture of our objectives goes to them.

There were many riflemen from A Company who, like Bettridge and Ross, had transferred to other units for one reason or another. Gordie Cole and Charlie McCaskill went to the anti-tank unit, Wilf Mercer to the flame throwers. Charlie Webber and Steve Agasse were in traffic control, and Dave Owen was in the Bren-gun carriers. Lieutenant Owen* was a real leader, kind and considerate; he listened to his NCOs and worked extremely well with the Boss. Jack Pond was now our A Company captain, second in charge, with Maj. Dick Medland as commander.

Jack Martin and Ben Dunkleman were old comrades in the mortar platoon. Back in England training days, we once had a particularly gruelling route march. Both Ben, a lieutenant, and Jack, a rifleman, had a hard time. Their feet were in bad shape, the blood running through their socks. Both refused to quit. "Nobody in 9 Platoon rides on a route march," they said. Anyway, I bandaged both and they were able to carry on.

Ben was always good for the unpredictable. You'd certainly never count him out. One other time, probably in December 1944, we had a four-day leave in England. Everyone was there for goodbyes at the train station as we headed back to Nijmegen, and of course Vi was there and we clung together pretty hard as time ran out. Almost at the last minute along came Ben. He had a half gallon of rum with him, and I don't think at that stage it was still completely full. He came up to us and gave Vi the most perfect salute in history. (If you knew Ben, you'd know how unbelievable *that* was!) He was filled with emotion, remembering, I suppose, what we'd been through over the previous six months. "It's an honour to meet you, M'am," said Ben, his voice shaky.

---

* Lieut. David Owen died of wounds August 18, 1944. His father, Archbishop Derwyn T. Owen, had also served in the Queen's Own and had visited the battalion at Shoreham the previous year. Archbishop Owen was primate of the Anglican Church in Canada.

That was a sad leave-taking. I started several times for the train but came back for "just one more." It nearly cost me the train, but I *just* made it – barely.

Now, with so much behind us, we of A Company experienced a great sense of loss for the QORs in our other three companies who had died. We had known many of them well, since the Queen's Own companies had trained together. And I'd met many while acting as instructor on many battalion courses – physical training, small arms, scouting, field craft, battle drill and so on. One other reason we had so many close comrades outside of A Company was that when a fourth unit – D Company – was created, our outfit had provided a complete platoon. A Company also contributed the unit's new commander, Lieut. Neil Gordon, and I had served with him for three years. Thus, when D Company suffered so badly at Le Mesnil-Patry on June 11, losing M.J. Quinlan (a corporal) and Bob Fleming (a lieutenant), we really felt we had lost our own A Company originals.

Despite the loss of Elliot Dalton, ten platoon commanders and many NCOs, all the rest took up the slack in just the same way as the ordinary riflemen on D-Day had stepped in when necessary to become acting platoon commanders. And the reinforcements at this time were more than excellent – contrary to many newspaper reports. These men had come forward to form a capable and brave new company, and they continued the excellent work of their earlier counterparts.

The Pursuit across France

After Falaise, action began again on August 23, 1944, as we took up the pursuit of a retreating enemy across the rivers and farms of France. A day or so later Jock Spragge was given a brigade command; Col. Steve Lett took over.

In our actions for about ten days or so, movement was difficult and the conditions in the August heat sickening. The roadside was cluttered with dead horses, vehicles and wagons. The bulk of the enemy army appeared to be horse drawn, we soon learned, and we saw, smelled and were revolted by the evidence. Burned trucks, tanks and hundreds of enemy soldiers and civilians lay thick among the horses along the hedges and roadsides.

The enemy retreat was orderly and well planned. They would hold for a day or two; we would tee up for our attack; but when we moved in, most would be gone. A few sacrificial prisoners were taken, but the main force were cleverly buying time at our expense in order to move back to new defence positions.

By now it was clear that our weapons build-up was overpowering. That the enemy did so well, that they could continue fighting under bombing from our heavies and machine-gun fire from both ground and air – well, it was a puzzle.

For example, time and again they'd hold a river for perhaps a few days. Then they'd just give it up and retreat to a new position. This did allow us to make a kind of progress but it was very trying all the same. And it was hard work. First off we would dig in and set up defences. That takes a lot of effort. You'd do this every few days. And the ever-present threat of their counterattack was hard on the nerves. These defences had to be good – you were never sure what to expect.

They were using good tactics, giving themselves time to rein-
force Nijmegen, which stood between us and the Rhine. The
heavy defence area they created caused the Allies problems that
have since been well documented in films and books.

All three of our platoons were now made up of 85 percent
reinforcements – men who had joined us after June 8 or later. On
the evening of September 4 we reached Lacapelle, a small village
outside of Boulogne. Then we moved up to Bois de Souverain
Moulin, ready for a full-scale battle to capture the much-needed
port of Boulogne.

Boulogne

The First Port
September 4, 1944, and the days following

After a steady diet of fighting at the rivers, in the fields or in the woods, we now looked upon a city that, located as it was on a very steep hill, had been turned into a fortress. Starting about September 4 and for about two weeks after, there were patrols, map studies and discussion.

In the preliminary days we took some really heavy shelling. One section of B Company suffered a direct hit. Art Richardson lost one leg and was badly injured in the other. In footraces back in England he'd been one of our three top runners in both the mile and cross-country, and he had been with us on D-Day. Art had caught hell on D-Day, he told me once, and it came from our own people. He and John Misson were in B Company. They landed left of the centre, reached the wall, but they had no ladder. They found a hole, got through and proceeded to clear the area. But they got a rocket from one of the officers because they'd dropped their haversacks on the beach and left them behind!*

The objective given to us on September 17 was the capture of an area outside of Boulogne called St. Martin, which contained a church and a railway station.

There were a number of unusual things in this action.

The enemy allowed the civilians to leave before our attack. As the people streamed out, we saw examples of more cruelty. Girls and women accused of collaboration with the enemy were being made to pay a price. From a distance we could see these poor

---

* Art Richardson survived and became president of the War Amps of Canada. He died in 1993.

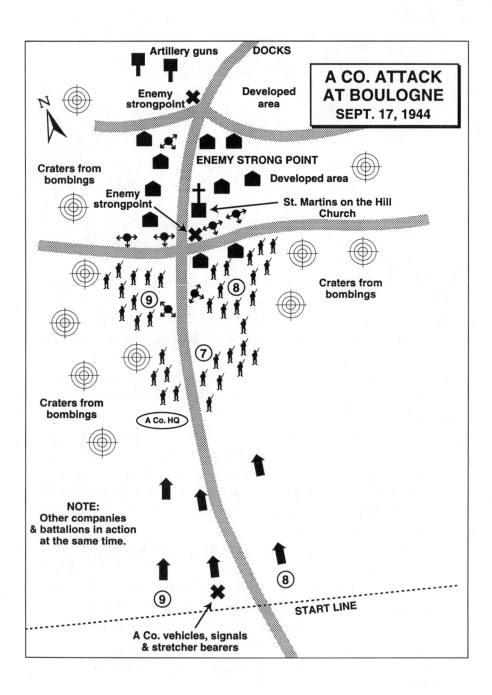

girls crying as other civilians used scissors to cut off all their hair. To me it seemed a brutal thing – just for a few dates with a lonely enemy soldier in some cases. I felt worse about that than the actual fighting.

Then, just before the battle someone had the idea that a platoon from the Lorne Scots should get some battle experience. They'd been defending Brigade and Divisional HQ up to this point, and this would be their first action.

Our battle plan called first for five hundred heavy bombers; they made two runs over Boulogne and the strong points outside. It was an awesome thing to see those machines. The bomb bay doors would open up the bellies of those things; flocks of bombs streamed downwards over our heads but continued on (we prayed) in a forward direction. One misfit actually did fall behind our holding line. We'd already seen the bombing accidents on August 14. I don't know what the others were doing, but my observations were made from the top of a good, stout, tall tree.

All weapons are capable of the unpredictable. Bombs, artillery, mortars fall short. A mortar bomb blows up an ammo dump. A soldier takes a direct hit. These create horrendous overkills. Even the best training cannot prepare a man for the strange, the odd or the impossible that actually does take place under battle conditions.

The bomb craters were enormous. They needed to be. The enemy had built concrete emplacements at tremendous depths. They had their belt-fed machine guns equipped with periscopes and mounted on elevator platforms. The automatic fire rate was huge, but the craters helped to spoil what would have been a perfect (for them) field of fire.

We had a road to follow; 9 Platoon took the left and 8 Platoon the right. We were under heavy shelling and machine-gun fire, but we were moving fast, zigzagging, changing speeds and being careful to be well spread out – from the point man at our front to the last section man, our coverage would be about a hundred yards. We were lucky to take only a few light casualties.

We got to the road junction near the top of the hill. They had the crossroads covered with heavy machine-gun and mortar fire. This fire pinned down both platoons.

The tanks were behind us, maybe a half mile down the hill, held up by craters and the mines. The sappers were working in the minefield using the Flails to create a path. These machines have a large sort of fly wheel about twenty feet in front, and they were blowing up mines as fast as they could find them. The noise was terrific. We knew they needed to get this done before we had any hope of reinforcement.

So we're at the crossroads – our 9 Platoon on the left and Joey Carmichael over on the right with a section from 8 Platoon – and we are in serious trouble. We had to get the machine gun that was holding us down. Jimmy Young went after it, followed by Steve de Blois.* Halfway across the road both were killed. Then Ernie Hackett and the rest of his section stormed across and got to the pillbox. We used our smoke bombs to choke them out. Ernie was badly wounded in the action and a number of others in 9 Platoon took wounds.

But 8 Platoon was having similar problems. They too were pinned down by heavy mortar and machine-gun fire. Cpl. Joey Carmichael bravely led his section across the road and took out the last machine gun. He was seriously injured in the leg. But now the rest of 8 Platoon could move across the road and take up a defensive position north of the church area. We were able to set up our A Company HQ in the house (manse) adjacent to the church. The wounded were gathered together in the church itself. The nuns took over the advance first-aid station, and the prisoners were gathered together in one of the outbuildings. The company was now consolidated on the objective in all-round defence and we reported this to Battalion HQ.

The Lorne Scots (now 7 Platoon) took up the frontal positions. Unbelievably – everyone had been under heavy mortar and

* Steve, Lomar and Alex de Blois were brothers from Cochrane – one in each platoon.

artillery fire all day – they were intact; if they were inexperienced in action, it sure didn't show. They held firm on the west.

The nuns who had stayed behind were full of tears. They were so compassionate; they even gave the boys a glass or two of wine. I hope they held back enough for the next communion, but our fellows didn't seem to worry about that at the time.

We could now review the problems at hand. The wounded were under good care with the nuns. The prisoners were under control; two guards could handle that situation. So ammunition and food got the number-one priority. And we figured the vehicles we'd use for that job could take out some of the wounded on their return trip.

It was almost dark. Charlie Bloomfield and I got ready to return to the start line to bring up the jeep and the Bren-gun carrier with all the support material we needed. This was pretty risky. There were still enemy positions around, shelling and firing small arms, and we had to pass through those minefields. So first we got on the walkie-talkie to Dick Klintworth to let him know we were on the way.

We needed something white to mark our safe trail out so that we could follow that path on the way back and avoid the mines. I approached one of the sisters who could speak excellent English. She gave me the most beautiful smile I'd ever seen and handed me the church supply of tablecloths and napkins, saying, "Our priest is giving a special prayer for you and your men."

When we got back to the start line, Dick was waiting for us. He had the carrier well loaded with a hot meal. And right with him we saw "Pops," the company's chief cook. I didn't know his age, but the nickname makes it clear he was well up on us.

I told him, thanks for the food, it's just great to have it, and we can manage things okay, so we'll be going.

"I cooked it, I serve it," was his answer.

Well, Dick Klintworth was to drive the carrier and W. Pennell the jeep. Pennell, in his typically outspoken way, argued that it was going to be very risky going up to the top of the hill again even though we had marked our safe trail. There was shelling, the minefields and some still very effective enemy forces holding positions behind the lines.

Dick kind of supported Pennell's views about the mines, but he finally settled the matter when he said, "Charlie will walk in front of us in the minefields, and where he leads, I follow." You'd have to know Klintworth and his mates in that tough Cabbagetown platoon. They didn't toss too many compliments around and that was a rare one.

So the group of us – Klintworth, Pennell, Bloomfield, Pops and I – started out in two vehicles. It wasn't easy, but we got through both minefields. It was only thanks to those white napkins and tablecloths from the church.

Well, it took a while, but by nine o'clock that evening, everyone had dug in, weapons were all cleaned, extra Brens and ammunition were in place, and Pops had served what seemed like the best meal any of us had ever had.

But it was still a tough night for some of us. The nuns and Slim Cole, our stretcher-bearer, were doing a good job looking after the wounded. But the Boss was very upset about the loss of Steve de Blois and Jimmy Young. They'd been with us in action since D-Day. Jimmy was a sergeant, very soft-spoken, and he had such a smooth and coordinated way of moving you'd actually think he was slow. He wasn't. At the Carpiquet airfield he took his men in to pick up our wounded. He'd shoulder-lift a man and get him out fast. And he could beat anyone in breaking down and reassembling the parts of a machine gun.

I guess all officers – and I know it's true for NCOs – feel the kind of responsibility the Boss did. You send out two point men; you know they may be killed or wounded and that you'll most likely see it happen. Commanders are surely plagued with the same thoughts when they send men into battle. This may explain why many leaders act as point men themselves – which they should not do except as a last resort.

Well, the night settled down and more prisoners still kept coming in. Then came the counterattack. It was in 7 Platoon's – the Lorne Scots' – area, but they were well dug in and succeeded

Many of the prisoners taken were very young. And they didn't always have the best training or tactics. They'd dig in at the centre of a field, for example, rather than at the perimeter or near a building where they might have some fallback route available. This young lad looks like he's had a bad few days.

Photo by F.L. Duberville, National Archives of Canada, PA 114495

This is one of the typical crossroads on the route from Caen to Falaise. Troops and vehicles are moving up. Likely this was one of the defended strong points. The farm buildings have been damaged by shelling and the fields all around are pock-marked by bomb craters.

This photo of our carrier was taken before our attack on Boulogne. Dick Klintworth is in his usual driver's seat, "Pops," the cook, is to the left, and I'm in the foreground.

While we waited and hoped for tank support, machines like this Flail would cover the ground and explode everything the whirling chains in front could touch. Then the tanks could have a safe path to get up to the riflemen on the objective.
Canadian Military Photograph

The hill at Boulogne, just on the way up to the crossroads that was covered by heavy machine-gun and mortar fire. Jimmy Young and Steve de Blois gave their lives here trying to take out the gun. The photo was taken in 1952.

This is at Nijmegen, some time near Christmas. In the centre is the Boss, Dick Medland, looking pretty dapper in those conditions, his ever-present cane in evidence just behind his right hip. Jack Pond, our captain and second-in-command, is on the right holding a good-sized pair of mitts. That's me, left.

The Canadian "Water Rats" in the 3rd Division fought through the Scheldt in areas like the one shown above. The dikes and houses were the only places to sleep or rest. One good thing – shells from the enemy buried themselves harmlessly in the mud; shrapnel could only hurt you from air bursts.

K-house in 1985 looked pretty peaceful. When we were there near the end of 1944, the hill behind the house contained all kinds of trouble. In this photo all the rubble, the outbuildings and the badly shelled barn have disappeared.

This photo was not taken until 1985, and the well with the pump handle are pretty much as they were when Bert Shepherd elected to let himself be heard from, more than forty years earlier.

Our mortar platoon was important to us as support for forward troops. Mortars were not an accurate weapon; instead they'd blanket an area with their fire – usually a pretty good way to cause some damage, crack morale and disrupt things generally. This one is a three-inch mortar. The bombs and carrying cases are alongside.
Captain Peter Simundson, CO, Queen's Own Rifles Museum

Captain Andrew J. Mowatt, padre for the Queen's Own Rifles. His face, wet with tears, was about the last thing I saw before slipping into a coma after being hit at Sneek.

A Sherman tank. The Hussars and Fort Garry Horse did a tremendous job of giving the QOR riflemen magnificent support; they would always make the extra effort. If supporting weapons are used to the best advantage, many times there are very few casualties; if not, look out. A leader had to make use of Typhoons and all his support companies – mortar, anti-tank, carriers, platoons, artillery, and if available, naval support.

Support company's anti-tank guns and their crews were the main defence in holding a village or woods against a tank attack. They were also very valuable in street fighting.
Photo be Ken Bell, National Archives of Canada, PA 132873

The enemy dynamited a major dike just before retreating farther east. Troops would often move in amphibious vehicles like these. This photo could have been taken in the Waal Flats.

Artillery support was important in both attacking and defending a position. It saved many riflemen's lives. Co-ordination usually depended on reports from the forward observation officer, who most often would be up with us, watching and correcting the fire.
Photo by Ken Bell, National Archives of Canada, PA 115569

This shot could have been taken in about the third or fourth week of February 1945 as we struggled through some terrible conditions, the mud being about the worst.

This shows a Bren-gunner prepared for action, with the second man ready to feed the extra magazines. You could get rid of twenty-eight rounds pretty quickly. This shot was taken by the famous (today) Ken Bell, and he's probably asked these two to push aside their camouflage to make the photo possible. Otherwise they are far too exposed.

Photo by Ken Bell, National Archives of Canada, PA 131417

One of our flame throwers in action – it takes about eighty feet or so before the fuel ignites. The Wasp's chief purpose was to cause fright or panic. The best way was always to find a method to persuade the enemy to give up and surrender. These weapons were pretty effective at discouraging opposition.

Canadian Military Photograph

This cartoon gets across what all of us thought. Bill Hill was a volunteer from over the border, one of those who heard the call early and came up to Canada. We called him "the Oklahoma Kid."

Coming home to a new life, a new start and a new world — on the hospital ship *Letitia*.

Yep, that's me. Grinning and on the way home. I had a lot to be thankful for, and a lot to be happy about, despite those crutches.

Vi Martin served for four and a half years as a radar operator on artillery sites in London, Essex, Sussex and Kent. Radar was effective in locating and tracking V-I and V-II bombs, which the artillery generally – not always – could then destroy in the air.

I didn't take the time to get rid of my hat, and the flowers look as though they weren't getting too much attention. I'd returned the previous August before Vi's discharge. She came in April 1946 on board the *Aquitania*. We headed straight for our little farm cottage in Dixie – $10 a month and no plumbing. Who complained?

in turning it back. I was with them at the time, maybe because they were our temporary replacements. I felt a little responsible, since so many were from our old towns and villages of Peel County – Brampton, Dixie, Port Credit and so on. Many prisoners were taken and the enemy were driven off.

Our company was not to get much sleep, as we'd been given instructions to hold for the night. Defence at night is wearing. Shadows move, gravestones shift. And anyone who believed there was truth in ghost stories had a real problem. In the early morning we prepared to move down to the city centre and the docks.

In our leader, Dick (the Boss) Medland, we had found the near-perfect commander. First, he listened to his NCOs and platoon leaders; second, he made every effort to tell each platoon commander the plan, specifically the objective for the company; third, any section could move on to the objective regardless of what happened to the others; fourth, he made a real effort to know each rifleman; and fifth – the most important – he let the section and platoon commanders lead their men. This meant he was always available at Company HQ or at Battalion HQ. It was easy for him to adapt to the nickname "Boss."

The Boss was now in a squeeze for the morning action. Our two platoons were down to half strength as a result of the previous long, hard day. So the decision was made to let the Lorne Scots – 7 Platoon – lead the attack. It was the morning of September 18, just at daylight. We had a very brave man, Lieut. J.D. Stewart, leading the platoon in absolutely the best fashion for street cleaning. There was a point man on the right side. Every time he moved forward, two men following twenty yards behind on the left gave him covering rifle fire. And twenty yards back again two Bren-gunners, one on each side of the road. As the point man moved up, so did one of the Brens – only one at a time – and when that small advance appeared secure the second Bren would come up. We seemed to be doing okay. There was some enemy fire coming in but it wasn't bothering us too much.

Suddenly a light machine gun vehicle appeared ahead. It opened fire immediately. Stewart jumped to his feet – he was always concerned about his men – and shouted for them to take cover. In the action that followed he was killed, probably by a sniper watching for officer material.

Jack Bennett (a sergeant in 9 Platoon) and I grabbed the Piat gun. Our first round missed, but we quickly got off a second bomb. That took out the vehicle, but not before we attracted some fire. Jack took a very bad one through the chest. It was almost unbelievable that our losses were not worse; that machine gun had been too close.

The Lorne Scots continued moving forward and took their objective. We were pretty proud in A Company to have them, and shared their grief in the loss of the platoon officer.

Innumerable prisoners were taken. One group were sailors – submariners we were told. Down the road they came in good marching order, a large white flag out front and a sailor with a mouth organ playing "Lili Marlene." The officer had a Nazi flag in his arms. It was folded specially, in the manner of a flag after a funeral. First he saluted me. Then in perfect English he said, "We surrender. And we are proud to surrender our submarine flag to the Canadians." It was amazing that these immaculate sailors, perfectly turned out, would do this. These navy people had a reputation as pretty good fighters. We were speechless. I still have this flag today.

Calais

Bombs Dug In and Wired
September 22 to October 1, 1944

Boulogne had been hilly country. At Calais the ground changed – lots of water and marshy territory. And there were more mines than at Boulogne and some of the most deadly traps we would encounter.

Prior to our advance on Calais, we had started to feel out the enemy with our usual patrols. Something very strange seemed to be going on. The patrols all came back with the same story – all quiet.

Dick Medland was concerned. These patrols had been led by Harold Clyne, Jack Boos and Jake Leather. These were our best patrol leaders – clever, experienced and diligent. They were not easily deceived. But "quiet" was a suspect answer.

There was no doubt these leaders had taken their patrols to the objectives stated in the orders. It did sometimes happen that a patrol might fall a bit short, or perhaps miss the order, or make a mistake in identifying the objective. We knew that couldn't be the case with these people. In any event, we planned one more patrol for the next evening.

We left at dusk in heavy rain – Charles Nahwegezhik, Josie Joslin, Charlie Bloomfield and myself. Charlie wore very thick eyeglasses, but by way of some compensation his hearing was unbelievable. We left Josie at the start point. The rest of us advanced well past the map reference point previously used, just trying to be sure. No noise except a dog barking. We withdrew and reported back to the Boss that up until about 9 p.m. no enemy had been seen in that area. So the Boss decided to go ahead. Next morning we moved forward for Calais with 8 Platoon in the lead.

There was heavy machine-gun fire, but no mortars or artillery. Bernie Bruyère, who had lost his brother on D-Day, was one of those quiet, unassuming fellows. He was the one who quickly observed that the fire was high in the air, uselessly pointing out towards the Channel. We got the idea the enemy no longer wanted to kill. And that's the way it was. They were ready to surrender and did in the hundreds. Our successful advance was achieved with very few casualties.

However, when we moved through the town of Calais itself, we discovered that the roads had been heavily mined. We ran into this again at the main intersection. These were unusual mines. What they'd done, apparently, was bury a number of heavy shells – the type artillery used against naval targets – and then wire them up by multiple methods so that a number of different things would set them off. First there were the trip wires. Releasing them would set off the charge. And tightening them would do the same. But to top it off they also had a temperature release detonator, an unusual type of trigger mechanism that was sensitive even to the heat of the hand. As soon as we discovered this one, we had Jackie Bland and Charles Nahwegezhik take some bed sheets from the house nearby and use them to rope off the area.

We asked Charles to stay behind and guard the spot. Then we sent a special message to Brigade HQ, by runner, asking for the engineers. After that the rest of us got back to other work.

About ten minutes later Charles came running for me at top speed. I knew something serious was wrong because he was shouting at me in Ojibwa. Normally Charles would be calm and unassuming. Even stoic and phlegmatic would not be too strong a description. He could see from my face that I couldn't understand him, and he tried to get hold of himself.

"Come on, come on – a jeep came up with an officer who wouldn't listen and he's trying to fix that bomb!"

"Well, you're the guard – didn't you explain things?"

"Yes, yes, I even cocked my rifle at him but he paid no attention at all."

I started running, Charles with me, because I knew how very dangerous that particular firing mechanism could be. If the engineers had arrived, they would have cleared the area and then blown up the bomb from a safe distance.

We'd no sooner started when we felt a huge explosion and then heard the noise. We were two hundred yards away but all kinds of debris rained down on us. Strangely, as if giving us a message, grisly body parts stood out in the mess around our feet. One had hair attached. We never learned who the officer and his driver were or where they came from. But they weren't Queen's Own.

Charles was from the reserve on Manitoulin Island. He'd been doing a wonderful job since coming up with reinforcements early in June. He was later wounded in an action on February 26, 1945, and it cost him his life. His heroic deeds were a credit to him.

For the Queen's Own, that was the end of the battle for the Channel ports.

To have served with these men was – well – just an unbelievable experience. Soldiers are many types – they pray, they cry, they get scared. And they get wounded and sometimes they get killed. The bravery we saw as they covered or assisted their fellow riflemen is beyond words. Nahwegezhik, Riddell, Collings, Brisbourne, McNab, Leather – all quiet, unassuming fellows – brought very special skills to every action.

And to balance up the world we had the characters and the cut-ups – Lennox, Bloomfield, Morgan, Bragg, Cargill, Dunstan and Kehoe. They had tricks and humour – as well as bravery – that surely helped keep us together. Now, after four months of action, our number was steadily shrinking.

In fact, at that date, of the 120 men who had landed in the first wave, we had only one officer, Jack Pond, still with us, and the list of remaining NCOs and riflemen would be as follows:*

Jack Bland
Charlie Bloomfield

---

* Dick Medland took over after June 11; otherwise he should be part of this list.

Jack Boyd
Ferdie Brisbois
Bernie Bruyère
Harold Clyne
Al Couroux
Bill Gruer
Jack Leather
Bill Lennox
Charles Martin
Percy McNab
Joe Meagher
Jim Morgan
Charles O'Brien
Jeff Oliver
Jim Smith, Jr.

That's one officer and seventeen other ranks out of 120. Makes you think.

Normandy, including Falaise, had been one long battle. The Channel ports just finished was another, different from Normandy. We had next in front of us the Scheldt Estuary, which would be different once again.

There was time at last for a rest. All the news from mothers, fathers, wives, sisters, brothers and friends would come in and it was always cheerful. I was lucky with a hefty collection of letters. There was a sizable pack from Vi, written every day. She was – as noted before – in the artillery helping to keep the skies clear over England. This was now the time of the buzz bombs. And I received letters from all of my sister's family, plus notes from Colonel Kennedy and Canon Banks.

As I've said, Canon Banks kept a special eye out for news of our A Company boys. Anyone lost would get a Sunday prayer. I passed around his letters to the others in our unit, and I'm sure they helped a lot. Everyone knew his support and concern were right with them.

In these rare rest periods we had time to collect ourselves and think. By now we all had developed great bonds of loyalty and affection for each other, and this was particularly the case among our shrinking group of D-Day originals. In the heat of battle you'd see things and not think too much about it. Afterwards, in these rest periods, some of the flashbacks would come to mind and you could only shake your head in wonder.

There are always stories about prisoners. I guess in the past and in the future there were and will be times when things get out of hand. With us, it never did. Even when a prisoner pulled a hidden weapon and fired at us, and we had every reason to strike hard, we did not. One we wounded a bit in the arm and leg – that was the action at Caen – and sent him back behind the line. Usually they were glad to give up. We sent them back with hands on heads, mostly with no guard. Sometimes if we had a wounded rifleman who could walk, we would use him as the guard; he'd be going back anyway. But most of the time we were too busy to spare anyone for guard duty. Generally they all looked like clean-cut people, young of course, maybe late teens to early twenties. And most spoke English, which was a help.

Only a very few showed any traces of the famous Nazi character. I encountered one on February 26, 1945, but we'll come to that later.

The Scheldt Estuary, Bresken's Pocket and the Battle of Oostburg

October 21 to October 26, 1944

The Queen's Own entered the battle for Bresken's Pocket in the Netherlands on October 12. We were riding in Buffaloes and crossing from the south side of the Westerschelde River. Buffaloes were amphibian vehicles for troop transport. If spotted by the enemy, they could be easily destroyed, especially when crossing water, since they were so big and could water-travel at only about 4 m.p.h. Any heavy wave action could also be disastrous. However, the crossing didn't seem to bother our men, even though the high winds and rough waters made our going, from my viewpoint, pretty risky. I guess by that stage of the game they could take almost anything. We safely made our landing at a bridge-head established earlier by the 9th Brigade.

Now we were again facing a completely different terrain. You'd have two or three farm buildings together and then up to maybe a half mile of open fields surrounded by dikes. Deep water had collected at the sides of the dikes, and it took courage for the men to move along them. There was no cover. It was what we called a section job. Each section – a corporal and a few riflemen usually – would leapfrog forward, advancing past the lead section. These attacks would take us from farmhouse to farmhouse. We'd do this five or six times a day – tense, stressful manoeuvres. You never knew what you'd be running into or what they might suddenly start to send your way.

At Boulogne and Calais we'd had high hills, bomb craters, streets and guns on a fixed line; in Normandy we'd had fields, hedgerows and roads. Now we were using ditches filled with water as our cover, and it wasn't much. As we moved deeper

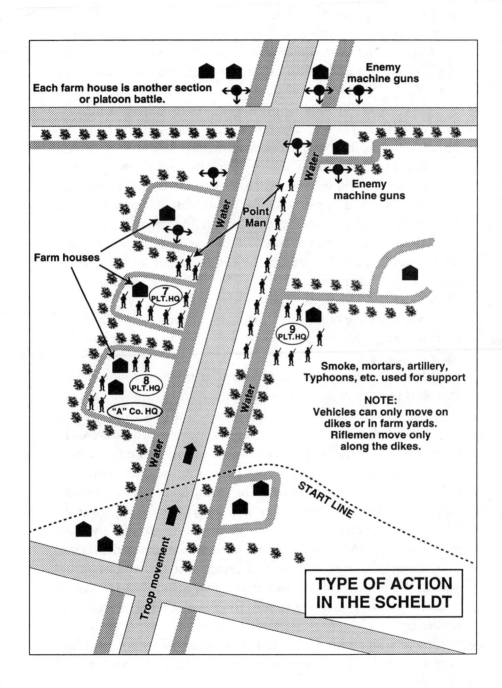

TYPE OF ACTION
IN THE SCHELDT

against the enemy, we were facing their regular army troops, not the teenagers in the Hitler Jugend or some others who had sometimes been thrown away at us while the key forces bought time.

As an example, we'd take an objective – a farmhouse let's say. We'd consolidate and hold. After a few hours, the shooting would start. The enemy were still there, hiding, waiting for their best chance to extract the highest price from us for their surrender.

Sometimes this was unintentional. There was the time, for instance, when Joe Meagher and a rifleman had dug in on the west side of a haystack. They were standing guard, watching to the west for any movement, when they heard an enemy weapon open up, real close. It seemed to be on the east side of their stack. So they dropped a grenade over. The firing stopped. They found two soldiers on the reverse side. One spoke English. After they'd been given first aid, he said that he and the other soldier had had no idea we'd taken our objective. They were just staying where they'd been put, doing their job.

But there were other incidents, more vicious, where they'd do their shooting, take their price and then just throw their hands in the air.

We were pretty experienced troops at this point, and overall managed to cope with these hazards. Experience, though, was not a complete answer to everything we would run up against. 8 Platoon had captured a small group of trees, a farmhouse and a barn. I had just come over to see about food and ammunition and to help pick up the wounded. There was a sudden barrage of heavy artillery and mortar fire. Our men, as usual, had already dug in and had fair cover. That was always the first step for us. Most of the shells were landing in very soft ground and just splashed mud and water around, so it was not too damaging. Still, it was a barrage and most of us had our heads down when we heard Bill Lennox and Jack Boyd, two of our most seasoned soldiers, shouting that the enemy from the other dike were surrendering.

It was a funny kind of surrender, starting off with a great barrage as it did. They were racing across the open wet ground towards us sure enough, but they were all carrying rifles. Then they began shooting. Some of our people had left their positions, curious to see what a bunch of "surrendering" soldiers looked like. We had three machine guns dug in and luckily two were still manned. We opened fire. Some of the attackers fell but the rest kept coming. I was right behind one of the slit trenches, and Ollie Burke was in there on the Bren. He was hit in the head and died instantly. I jumped in and took over the gun. The other two Brens were on automatic fire, and we had some rifle support. Suddenly they quit – just dropped their weapons and threw their arms in the air.

The amazing thing was how quickly, after the first call about the "surrender" and our moment or two of being deceived, everyone had jumped to their positions and opened the firing. For a day or so afterwards, Lennox and Boyd had to put up with some pretty heavy jokes at their expense.

From then on, there were three or four small battles a day. Usually it was section work; sometimes a platoon. It was crawling, dashing, rolling, three to five hundred yards for each battle, with an enemy in every haystack, house, barn, pigpen, chicken house and outbuilding. The greenhouses had most of their glass blown out, but the three-foot lower wall made ideal shelter from enemy machine-gun fire. But we took several casualties every day. And at that rate A Company was down to half strength and each section down to only six or seven men when we came to the battles for Ijzendijke and Oostburg.

In the battle for Ijzendijke, 7 Platoon ran into heavy machine-gun fire from across the town square. It was coming from a heavily sandbagged house with a big, solid, black door.* Dick Medland viewed this as real trouble. He chose our 9 Platoon to swing around and try to get behind the enemy position.

At this stage 9 Platoon had lost two successive commanders,

---

* The house and door are still there, or were in 1989 when Charlie Martin advised the bus group he was travelling with: "Around this next corner watch for the heavy black door."

two NCOs and a lot of wounded riflemen. But nonetheless we set about the job, planning carefully. We would move cautiously, travelling behind the dike whenever we could. 7 Platoon would hold in one of the houses on the east side of the square and supply covering fire for us. At the same time, 8 Platoon would move to the left and give us more covering fire. As soon as we got the objective, they'd move up.

We asked for fifteen minutes of heavy mortar bombing right behind their position in the house. We took our two-inch mortar with us. Its outstanding use was for smoke rather than explosives. While our support mortars could provide the same thing, along with shells, and regularly did so with consistently good results, this action was a very close attack kind of thing and we needed to carry the smoke bombs with us.

To get at this troubling gun position in the square, we had a section with Jake Leather, Jack Morgan, Bob Dunstan, Fred Brisboise, Drew Kehoe, Joe Parsons and myself. Dunstan and I took Sten guns. We all carried four grenades each.

We moved on the dead quiet, taking advantage of any concealment. And we had our smoke, which we hoped would hide us and blind them. There was no firing from them, and we were lucky enough to get behind the house without being seen.

Our plan called for Jack Morgan and Drew Kehoe to break in at the back door right after Dunstan and I went in through the back window. Dunstan popped a grenade through. After the explosion I dove in, rolled left and came up spraying the Sten left; Dunstan followed me in, rolling right and emptying his Sten. At almost the same moment Morgan and Kehoe burst through the door firing their Brens from the hip.

When the smoke had cleared – mostly plaster and dust – and hundreds of bullets later, all we could hear was "Kamerad." There were only three of them. And out of all this, aside from some minor flesh wounds, no casualties.

Kehoe found a white sheet and hung it out the window very, very carefully. He knew 7 Platoon were covering us and didn't want any misunderstandings. Then we fired off a green flare. It was our signal to tell the Boss at HQ that all was clear.

Sometime during this action I picked up a piece of shrapnel in the left shoulder. It's there yet. Slim Cole, our Newfoundland stretcher-bearer, put a bandage on it. Around this time Bob Carlow, a driver of one of the carriers, came up to see how the mortars had done and where the next lay-down might be needed. He told us of losing three carriers: one had run over a mine, one was hit by a shell in a farmyard, and one was disabled on a dike. Fortunately, Bob was not injured in any of these hits.

When we got to Oostburg, our company was given the job of feeling out enemy defences. We used 9 Platoon again. One section went forward with two lead men at the point, prepared for fire and movement. They were getting near a row of houses, still with two hundred yards to go, when enemy guns hidden in the buildings opened up. Our men were using a ditch well lined with trees and shrubs for concealment. Several riflemen were wounded; the lieutenant, E.E. Ottaway, was killed.

The section continued to hold under artillery, mortars and machine-gun fire but it was impossible to move forward unless we had a major assault. The men had done their job, locating not only an enemy but a very strong one, so they withdrew to our original position to await orders.

So a battalion attack was planned. Dick Medland called an O Group. He explained that our number-two carrier with the large signal set would control all the support. This would include artillery, mortars and Typhoons. And the flame throwers would be standing by if required. B Company would be getting in their attack at the north end of the town and C Company would hold our start line. D Company would move forward with us, and the Chaudières would be holding the area to the south.

This system of company control started after Normandy. Dick would be with the carrier; the jeep and its driver would be standing by; all the stretcher-bearers, signalmen and other vitally important support people would be on the job. We wanted no more signal sets strapped to a soldier's back. What a target! So this system for communications and control was a lot better.

Civilians sometimes think people at a headquarters area like this are just standing around holding the coats of those who go out to fight. They overlook the fact that this is precisely the area any sensible enemy would target. Get the nerve centre, get the brain. So HQ was no picnic. But we riflemen depended on them. A good, effective, reactive headquarters staff saved our lives many times over.

In this attack there was not too much cover available. Jack Boos and his 8 Platoon led. Jack was another new lieutenant who had been promoted from the ranks. Each of the other platoons provided covering fire from the flanks. About a hundred yards away from the first houses in the town stood a farmhouse. The point men and the section captured it. Jack and Jackie Bland with 9 Platoon moved forward with the rest to consolidate the whole area – buildings, hedges and overall about two acres. Then they sent back a runner to report on what they'd done.

I went back with the runner intending to explain how we meant to go after the houses in the town. B Company was on the other side of the village causing the enemy trouble. We felt we could now bring up 7 Platoon and together we'd advance to take over enemy positions in the houses just ahead.

It was not to be. Just as I arrived they had already started their advance. And of course who was with them? The commander, Jack Boos. Nonetheless it turned out to be a classic example of good riflemen at war.

They had crossed halfway to the houses when the enemy opened up. Then we saw men in action at a speed that was unbelievable. Nobody moved straight ahead. It was left and right. Up and down. Down and roll right. Fire. Then up again. Roll left. Fire. The action was perfect in its timing.

While this was going on, Jackie Bland had 9 Platoon on the road or in the ditches by the sides of the road, and they were giving covering fire. The runner and I, not part of all this, took a moment out of the war to watch in fascination. It was a wonderful example of an assault, with our men supporting each other in a clever coordination of movement, fire and flanking fire. By the time we got up to them, they had the objective. Out came the white flags. All they had were minor casualties.

As soldiers fight together day after day, action after action, they develop a special sense. They get to the point where they can read the battle. They can anticipate what should come next, how and when. It's a battle sense. And that's what we saw at Oostburg, with 8 Platoon assaulting and 9 Platoon supporting.

The consolidation process for Oostburg began right away. Prisoners were sent back. Then within minutes the enemy artillery began to come in.

Norm Mennard was with John Barrett when an 88 slammed into their brick wall. John was killed. Norm was wounded in the legs and arms, and his steel helmet went flying. Then the bricks came tumbling in. Just as he reached for his helmet a brick banged him on the head. He stayed conscious just long enough to jam the helmet back on. When he came to, almost buried in bricks, all he could see was me, the stretcher-bearer and the jeep standing by to take him out. He lit into us about how painful the falling bricks had been, not realizing he had also been badly wounded.

The stretcher-bearer wasn't having any of that.

"The government saved the cost of the first shot of morphine thanks to a brick; now here's a real one for you just in case there are no more bricks."

It took a while to dig him out of that mountain of rubble, but eventually off he went to the battalion's first-aid station and to those wonderful doctors and nurses.

And we went on to the last pillbox.

The Last Pillbox at Bresken

And Joe Meagher's Wound
November 2, 1944

To the north of Westcapelle we encountered a very strong position. It was a specially built pillbox, designed like a house and let's say about thirty by forty feet. Its walls were three feet thick, and it was encircled by concertina wire ten feet high and about a yard or so deep. On top of that, it was surrounded by a complete minefield and there were booby traps everywhere.

Worst of all, as we later discovered, we were encountering our first absolutely determined, dedicated Nazi SS officer. And he had a Gestapo officer with him (they had a tendency to rat on each other, which stiffened the backbone in each of them). This situation certainly made things a lot tougher, as it turned out.

We could have skipped it, waited them out or called for artillery or Typhoons, but for some reason the Boss was given this objective. They wanted it taken out. Once again Dick Medland had a tough decision. If we tried flanking to the left or to the right, we'd need to get through the minefield and blow up or cut up the wire. That meant we'd have to expose the demolition team for too long. It takes time to cut or explode wire, and they'd have us well covered by those belt-fed machine guns. And the wire might be booby trapped. Nobody wanted to choose that form of suicide.

Then somebody reported to the Boss that the wire gate, which should have closed off the roadway, was not in place. We checked with the binoculars. The road looked solid. One thing about roadways: they always had a hard surface and were not usually mined. If they were, the mines would be too obvious. This was a tarmac road with no signs of disturbance.

The position had already been pounded by our artillery and mortars. We had called in the Typhoons. No damage, or not much anyway, and no sign of surrender. So we decided once again that it would have to be a section job. And we decided to go straight at them, right down the roadway. A section from 7 Platoon was drawn up – Joe Meagher, Percy McNab, Charles Nahwegezhik, Red Simpson (the brother of my friend Jack, my seat-mate in the LCA during the D-Day landing), Bernie Bruyère, Jack Wilson, Charlie Bloomfield and me. As soon as we hit the gate marker, 9 Platoon's No. 8 section would jump in and follow up, ready to finish the job if we failed.

The Boss called first for heavy shelling to drop right on the objective. I had mixed feelings about that, having seen so much fire fall a tad short – it's supposed to fall on them, not us. Anyway, the nine of us got ready. We sent out the two point men with Joe on the left and Bernie on the right and the rest of us spread out. We were on both sides of the road, spaced, running fast and making ourselves as difficult targets as possible. The moment we hit the gate our artillery stopped – perfect timing.

But now we had to cover open ground to get close enough to drop in our grenades or smoke bombs, and we could still have used that shelling, maybe, to keep their heads down. But you can't have it both ways. So we're all running at top speed and once again the miracle we prayed for happened. Out from all the slits in the strong point came the white flags. They had surrendered. The battle for Bresken was won.

Our men were tired, soaking wet and cold. They'd seen steady action for a month. There'd been no sleep – just an hour here and there for a nap. Our outfit had shrunk to three very small platoons, but these riflemen had performed wonders. And as always, even in the midst of all the tension at the pillbox, something funny happened.

The nine of us were sitting down to catch our breath while the others took care of the prisoners. Joe Meagher, a rifleman in the Miners who had been promoted to sergeant, believed in super safety. He always wore his helmet. His slit trench was always very well covered with a strong roof. This was a very careful fellow all round. After the charge he was gasping and panting and streaming with sweat. We were all dripping with it, and to this day I don't know if it came from heat or fear. He took off his helmet to wipe away the perspiration. Just at that moment part of a clay shingle fell from the roof and cut his head. Joe swore he'd never take his helmet off again.

Laughter – crazy with relief. We had just finished an attack where we'd expected to lose a good part of our section and maybe the same for 9's No. 8 section, and all we had was a minor head casualty.

They took us to a farm south of Knocke. There we were fed a glorious hot meal and – with no enemy now within miles, no 88s or Moaning Minnies – we bedded down in warm, dry hay. Wonderful!

The next thing I remember was feeling as though I was coming out of a deep, dark pit. Charlie Bloomfield and Ernie Freelen were shaking me. They thought I was dead. They'd checked for pulse – couldn't feel anything – my eyes wouldn't open and they couldn't detect any breathing. They'd even called for the stretcher-bearers. It's just an example of how dragged out and dead tired we all were.

One rifleman from Northern Ontario who was with us at that time had a particularly unlucky wound; the doctors removed a testicle. Years later, in 1963, he called me to say he was having trouble with his war pension. Vi and I drove up to see him. He said he was only getting a 50 percent pension and felt he deserved more. Well, there were six children in the house. I couldn't stop myself from saying there didn't seem to be a really serious problem, but nonetheless I agreed to help him make the arrangements necessary for a pension board hearing.

"You seemed to have no trouble producing six children," they commented at the hearing.

Absolutely deadpan, he told them that but for his wound he would have had twelve.

They gave him another 10 percent.

And we were lucky to have Dick Medland. He never let things get him excited, and he was always available to us at HQ, where he needed to be. Some would wander about and interfere with the various activities section leaders might have on the go. Not Dick Medland. As long as we understood the objective, he let the platoon commanders and NCOs do the job. And this sometimes was not an easy thing. There is stress and tension at HQ as well as at the point, and commanders have to struggle with the knowledge that once the action is commenced, they have no further control. That's probably why some men consistently would refuse promotion, knowing they could not live with that kind of responsibility and discipline.

The battle for the Scheldt and Bresken's Pocket eventually became one of the Queen's Own battle honours. I remember it as a section job – two or three riflemen at a time, house after house, day after day. We had lost three platoon commanders and many others. All the actions in the polders, at the dikes and in the farm buildings or towns were a rifleman's fight. A section of men below the dike would slog along waist deep in water, watching their lead man near the top of the dike. He is the bait, the point man, as they sought to find the enemy. Sometimes he made it safely, sometimes he took a wound, often a bad one, and sometimes he was killed.

That's why no award for such men could be too great.

Support
Mortars, Carriers and Anti-tanks

The rifleman is always the first to go in. The foot soldier is the sharp edge of the sword; they take the first casualties. But they get (and need) tremendous support. Our mortar platoon, anti-tank platoon and Bren-gun carriers were always right there. The anti-tank gunners could elevate and drop fire directly on enemy emplacements anywhere – hidden in towns, farms or dug in. All we had to do was find them. And the Bren-gunners could supply us with the right cover fire.

Our mortars, as we found out later, were best set up in farm-yards in the lane, or driveway, which was the firmest ground available. And sometimes firm ground could be found behind a stone wall, which was almost ideal. But in the beginning our mortars men struggled in the soggy ground. A mortar has a base plate and the accuracy depends on the correct alignment, which is very tough in mud. So, being uncertain of their accuracy, they now needed an observation man up on the dike.

Mortars are very effective in breaking down the enemy nerve, or in keeping their heads down while we riflemen moved up to their position. The enemy know this and as a consequence are quick to identify the observation post and smear it with machine-gun fire. And they were equally quick to locate the sup-port mortars. So our mortar people – guys like Carl Warner, who was the sergeant commanding the section, and riflemen Jack Martin, Bill Ross, Jack Nicol, Charles McCaskill, Gord Cole, Danny McInnis – attracted a lot more of the enemy artillery attention than would other areas.

We relied heavily on our mortar support, and they always stood by us. One night* things were particularly bad. We had taken a strong point when the order came to drop back. Two of our platoons were already on the move up. We had to get our other platoon off the objective. Some of the men were trapped in a minefield; in a situation like that, in the dark, you can be overcome by a paralysis, afraid to make a move. And enemy artillery fire was coming in on us. It was a very mixed-up situation. A lot of men in A Company were on the move, or where they shouldn't be, and we badly needed the mortar support while we got things organized.

Our support kept pouring in the fire till the barrels were red hot. Somebody said maybe they should break off, let the guns cool. Shells could explode on contact at that temperature.

"Can't do it," somebody said. "Keep firing. A Company's out there and needs everything we can give them."

Generally most of our injuries – and the enemy's too – came from shrapnel after the explosion. These wounds were damaging, but usually clean. Some of the wounds from other weapons were on the nasty side; the tank men in particular would get very bad burns – terrible. The tank men always had my sympathy.

---

* November 29, 1944.

The Nijmegen Bridgehead

Taking Over from the 82nd Airborne
November 12, 1944, to February 1945

We had eight delicious days of rest in the city of Ghent. Then came the move to the area around Nijmegen. Some thought it would be a piece of cake.

Some cake.

Anyway, we were there for three months and had a chance to bring ourselves up to strength. Our fellows after the fighting in the Scheldt were pretty well worn out – battle weary and just plain tired.

When we took over from the Americans – it was the famed 82nd Airborne – we had to put up with some of their wisecracks. To begin with, their platoons were larger than ours. Theirs might consist of fifty men; ours of maybe thirty-two. But at that point, as we weren't up to strength, our platoons each had only about eighteen survivors.

So these paratroopers probably had some right to look at us pretty sceptically. They looked well fed to us, had nicer uniforms and all the canteen comforts, and for these guys to turn over their hard-won position to a platoon of eighteen tired-out and scraggly Canadians must have seemed a little ridiculous.

"Give us a call when the SS come back!"

"Let them back in here and you'll be hearing from us!"

Those were the sort of taunts they tossed our way as they left. They didn't know they were talking to some of the bravest and most capable riflemen in the war.

Anyway, in taking over from the 82nd, we found they'd dug a trench system on one of the hills similar to what was done in the first war. The trench was a good ten feet deep – probably they had in mind the double purpose of a tank trap – and they had a really neat footstep for the lookout. There two listening posts down in the valley, about four hundred yards out. One was called K-house, the other C-house.

On our first night after we'd moved up, half of 9 Platoon were detailed to meet the paratroopers at K-house and I went with them. We found only three troopers and they were very insistent about maintaining a complete silence.

We didn't much like what we saw. The three of them had their equipment in a root cellar and the telephone wire just lay in the field. An enemy soldier could easily get around the house at night and simply cut the wire. And of the three, only one was on guard upstairs. If there was any kind of attack, they'd have to be very lucky not to have a cut wire and a quick overrun. The enemy had a clear view of us. That's why the paratroopers had decided not to make any noise or do any digging. They thought maybe they were undetected.

We didn't care for it at all. This, after all, was no man's land. We had too much hard-earned respect for the enemy; without better defences our men could be destroyed or captured any time.

Bruyère and I made ready to get back to the Boss for some instruction, but first we ignored the American advice and started Jake Leather and his section digging four slit trenches around the house. When we returned to HQ, we were glad to learn that Dick Medland shared our concern and supported us.

So he sent us back, as well as three others (Keeton, Barrett and Kehoe), along with two Piat guns, bombs, flares, trip wires and extra grenades to tie to them, two extra Brens, sandbags, and a walkie-talkie to supplement the field telephone. Those paratroopers would have had heart failure if they had been there to see all this hardware moving up and to hear the noises (some, anyway) that went with it.

We spent the next few hours of darkness strengthening the position. Naturally the enemy heard something going on and mortared and shelled us several times. But we now had some good cover, though we were still not too happy with it. Since we had to get back before dawn, further improvements would have to wait. I returned with the relief group after dark the next night and watched Jake and his section get out for twenty-four hours' rest. They were glad to leave, knowing they would be out of K-house for six whole days; then the rotation system would put them back in again.

We brought still more equipment with us – barbed wire, more flares and grenades, and more ammunition. Another night's work was put in, including a tunnel out of the root cellar. Now K-house at least had some decent protection.

It was still cold and wet. And we still had the enemy 88s and 75s coming at us. Maybe the Moaning Minnies were worst. They weren't accurate at all, but could spread all kinds of metal junk over a wide area. And the horrible screaming noise they made coming in could break anyone's nerve. We'd try to locate the Minnie and knock it out. But every few minutes they'd hook the thing to the back of a carrier or something and move it some-where else. So our return fire was too late. The enemy soldiers would still be in the target area, so they must have cursed the Moaning Minnies as much as we did, knowing what always came afterwards.

The tension was great. You never knew when enemy fire would be coming. Off to our right a section of C Company held, appropriately, C-house. One night they were overrun. The officer was wounded and the section taken prisoner. The next night other sections of C Company counterattacked, and C-house was once again theirs, but the prisoners were lost. The lieutenant and a rifleman were wounded and all were taken to Germany for the rest of the war.

After some days of this kind of thing, we had done a lot with our defences. One night about two in the morning, I came up to see how things were. Ernie Freelen was with me. With our rota-tion system, this was a night when Harold Clyne and some oth-ers from 7 Platoon were manning the post. They were all wide awake; K-house was not a place where anyone could even nap, let alone sleep. There was McNab, Caverley, Gardiner, Nahwegezhik,

Riddell, Bradshaw, Bragg and maybe six others. By this time I couldn't keep track of all the new reinforcements. It was a big effort even to remember their last names.

I'd no sooner arrived when our flares went up and we heard a vehicle coming. Enemy mortar shells rained down for about ten minutes. Then a heavy machine gun opened up.

Suddenly everything stopped. Now we again heard the vehicle approaching. They hit our outside perimeter flares. The scout car or whatever it might have been was moving towards us rapidly. We heard a shout: "Canadians, surrender or you will die." The scout car was now sixty yards away, firing and moving in fast.

Everyone was firing. The racket was tremendous. Outside, the mines were exploding and we could tell the trip wires were being activated. About the only thing to do when you know something's coming is to blast away with everything you've got. We did that with a vengeance.

One of the Piat guns was resting on the sandbags that plugged up the windows. I loaded the Piat with a bomb. According to the manuals, you're supposed to handle those things in a certain way, from a prone position. There was no time for that. I just fired it off. The gun's recoil hit me smack in the face – knocked me right back through the one brick wall still standing. My nose bled like a stuck pig. Ernie Freelen sat there grinning like an ape. He thought it was a big laugh. My first thought was that Ernie had at last gone nuts, but then realized the enemy had turned tail and retreated. Ernie had time to relax himself at my expense.

They'd gone. We weren't sure why. There was so sign of anything – no wrecked vehicles, no dead or wounded to be seen. I like to think that they just couldn't stand up to the fire 7 Platoon gave them. In the ten-minute engagement we had fired hundreds of rounds, ten Piat bombs and I don't know how many grenades.

Our artillery support helped, too. We'd called for that on the telephone. Most of it was to the front but some came in on us. Again it was time to be amazed – no real casualties, just a few bruises and slight wounds.

The next few days were quiet, or reasonably so. Every night the men spent time improving the defences. They knew that in a real counterattack, there wouldn't be much hope for them. But the enemy had been driven off from K-house once. They knew they'd have a fight on their hands if they came again.

During this time I always tried to scout around a bit most every night. But daylight patrols were my choice. If you used ground and cover carefully, they shouldn't see you. And it developed that if only one or two were out in no man's land, the enemy seldom fired, possibly deciding to protect their position rather than give themselves away for such a low price.

The Day Bert Shepherd Kept Quiet

One day in the early morning, I went out to pay a call on Bert Shepherd. He had a concealed observation post and I was just checking to make sure everything was alright.

Well, Bert had something on his mind. He had the notion maybe the enemy were just playing around with him, not taking him seriously or something like that. What was getting under his skin in particular was the casual way they went for water. Every morning, he told me, one of the enemy soldiers on the opposite hill would grab his bucket and stroll brazenly to the pump, fill the bucket and stroll back again. Bert wanted to put a bullet in him; he felt such conduct was just their way of twisting his nose. Bert was not one to put up with very much, and he'd had about enough of such insults from them.

I tried to talk him out of it. I said the range was pretty far, too far to be sure of the shot. More than that, he'd just stir up trouble for us. The quiet time we were having might be long gone.

I left him knowing that he was still stewing about the high-handed treatment he felt he was getting from them. Actually I needed to leave because the call of nature was suddenly too strong. Our boys had built a rather elaborate toilet stacked safely with sandbags and well away from the house in the rubble of the outbuildings.

I'd just got there when I heard Bert squeeze off his shot. I groaned. Boy, did we catch a barrage – Moaning Minnies again with lots of 88s. It came almost instantaneously, just as if Bert the volunteer stage manager had given the cue. Luckily nothing was hurt except our feelings.

I asked Bert about it later. He had to confess that the distance was too much. All he'd been able to hit was the bucket and the pump handle. He sure learned a few new words from some of us. For about ten minutes he had no friends at all. After I'd unloaded on him he was strangely silent. It was about the only time I'd ever seen him shut up.

The Waal Flats at Nijmegen

A Minefield in the Dark
November and December 1944

About November 22 we moved to a new area south of the River Waal. The weather as always was cold and wet. We were asked to hold some low ground called the Waal Flats, an area about ten square miles. Our slit trenches kept getting wetter and wetter from the rising water. Patrols were difficult and we had a lot of them. One night we spent four hours stalking an enemy patrol coming in. Their "patrol" turned out to be six sheep. We had mutton for supper.

Our reinforcements were good. In fact, they were as good as their instructors. Action is a place where you learn fast or you're gone.

Around this time the rumour got going that the Canadian High Command had plans for a large-scale attack to clear the Waal Flats. Then the rumour began to shrink. It was only to be a regimental attack. Then it became a company attack, mainly to cause a distraction. Then it came down to us raiding a strong point at the crossroads.

Our attack started at dusk on November 29. Jack Boos was in charge. The idea was for 8 Platoon to move up to the crossroads, which were really a cross-dikes, then for 7 Platoon to move in from the left under Harold Clyne and Percy McNab. 9 Platoon was in reserve. 8 Platoon got the strong point eventually. But when 9 Platoon made ready to move up and consolidate, the enemy opened up with heavy machine-gun fire from another position.

A signal came in that the attack had been called off. But now we had the strong point already in our possession and two of our

platoons (7 from the left and 9 from the rear) were in the process
of moving up to consolidate the objective. The whole area was
heavily mined and we were also taking heavy artillery fire. Then
we discovered that several of our men in 8 Platoon were trapped
in the minefield. Jack Boos was with them and he had been seriously wounded.

Though the order for us to drop back rather than to dig in
and hold was correct, we had the problem of how to get everyone
back. We needed to make contact with 7 and 9. We needed to
pick up our wounded and make sure everyone was taken care of.
It was pitch-dark and Jack was out there in terrific pain. I got to
him, crossing the minefield in the dark – luck again – and gave
him morphine. It didn't seem to do the job, so I gave him a second shot. That helped, but it put him out. His 160 pounds
became a dead weight. Fireman's lift again.

I signalled to the other men and they followed my trail out.
Ernie Freelen was waiting for me. He had led the Bren carrier
through the mines with Dick Klintworth doing the driving. They
had ammo, water and stretchers with them. Jack and the other
wounded were in a first-class field hospital before dawn.*

Now we had to get on with the rest of it. We asked 8 Platoon
to stay and hold the objective till we'd made contact with the
other two platoons and had figured out a way to get them back
to our start line. I debated about sending a runner.

I knew where 7 Platoon should be. A runner, however, might
not be able to find them. And if he did, he might not succeed in
convincing guys like Clyne and McNab to fall back. Once they
had an objective they liked to hold come hell or high water. So I
made ready to go myself. I asked them to give me fifteen minutes, then fire the signal – a green and red flare – for the drop
back. A green flare meant OK; a red flare meant trouble; green
and red together meant drop back.

---

* Charlie didn't see Jack Boos again until 1952. He had lost the use of both legs and
his wife did the driving out to the Martins' farm in Dixie. It was an affectionate, tearful
reunion.

That's about how long it took me to find Harold and two sections of 7 Platoon. McNab, though, had already moved forward with three others; they were checking out the next position. I knew Harold would stay right there till he heard from me, so I took off after McNab. I quickly found his lookout, J.A. Riddell, at the point of entry where their tape into the minefield began. Finding where the rest of them were would be difficult. McNab had Brunet and Nahwegezhik with him, and they would probably be out there till nearly dawn, figuring no problem, their platoon mates were still behind them firming up the position.

Just as I began to follow their tape, the enemy sent up a barrage of flares and artillery. I froze in the ghostly light, just as you're supposed to do, and then jumped a foot as I saw a man on the ground in front of me. I thought it was a dead McNab. Then with relief I saw the enemy uniform.

Eventually I located them and gave my code word. Many of our men kept changing theirs. That was something you had to be very careful about. Different code words could be forgotten and that might lead to trouble. I always used my Christian name initials, "CC," and everyone recognized that.

Dawn was about to break when we made it back.

Now with a new day we expected a counterattack. Everyone stood to at their posts. We called for the heavy artillery and Typhoons. They blasted away at the enemy's second line, which had been pinpointed in the observations of the previous night. Sure enough, these Typhoons made the difference; our later ground attack succeeded in clearing the area.

About this time instructions had come along for us to make contact with the Régiment de la Chaudière. For some reason we were placed out towards the enemy positions, and so in moving back we made a very careful approach so as not to be misidentified. Suddenly we heard a chorus of song in a foreign language from behind us. The language alone was enough to throw us into our defensive positions immediately. Along came a happy section of Canadian soldiers, rifles over their shoulders and each with a jaunty American helmet – and all in chorus at top voice.

Bernie Bruyère shouted to all of us, "They're French – hold your fire!" It turned out they were Chaudières who had penetrated goodness knows how far into the enemy's territory, far enough anyhow to stumble across a wine supply which they'd liberally sampled. Bernie took them back to our cookhouse and sobered them up with hot food and coffee. We guided them back to their position and kept our mouths shut. Those Chaudières had made themselves very happy for a time, but they were lucky not to have encountered something more serious.

Holding Nijmegen in those cold winter months was tough. But there was time for some of the men to get a four-day holiday. And, of course, we had the chance to bring the company up to strength, ready for the next big push. We had lost all our platoon commanders in this period, so three new officers arrived as reinforcements in January and February. All our replacements of other ranks fitted into their platoons very well within weeks. The knowledge imparted from the old veterans of eight months was absorbed like a sponge. Most of the new men were paired up with the more battle-scarred veterans.

War is very tiring – not enough sleep, tension from high explosives, fear of counterattack, the tough work of patrols, the attacks from ditch to ditch, house to house, bush to bush, heavy machine-gun fire and nerves stretched beyond human endurance. And the risk and tension in the minefields bring a fear no one can explain in words.

And yet, despite some of the newspaper accounts at that time, we saw nothing but courage in both our old-timers and new men. They had nerve and grit. I believe this courage came from love – love for family, comrades and country. Beyond that, it has always been a kind of mystery exactly how it happens that ordinary human beings can act so bravely and selflessly.

Every decoration awarded within A Company could have been awarded to anyone. In fact, sometimes it seemed the bravest were not recognized at all. Often a man operating alone would do something really amazing and live to tell a tale sometime afterwards that could stun you. But since nobody had been there to see it, a deserved decoration would go unrecommended. Anyone who served in a front-line rifle company for two months would have done enough to get a decoration. Two months in a rifle company meant you were well trained, careful, observant, quick – and damn lucky. And a few prayers probably helped.

We did not know it at the time, but some of our most terrible battles were yet to come. The break-out to capture the Rhineland and get over the river into Germany would cost yet more in life and limb.

In the Rhineland

Teacups and Rum
February 8, 1945

The enemy's first line of defence was the Siegfried Line, the Hochwald and the Balbegerwald (town of Bogelkath). The Allied advance had been and was to capture the Waal Flats, all the dikes, the River Waal and the town of Milligen; this had to be done before moving south towards the city of Cleve.

On February 8, 1945, we began our attack to clear the west side of the Rhine. The first job for A Company was to capture part of Milligen and the dikes west of town. An especially large dike, meant to keep the water from the River Waal from flooding Millegen, had been blown apart by the enemy. The water consequently had come in and had kept rising until the only way to get about was by boat.

One night after we were consolidated, the enemy foolishly sent a patrol by boat to investigate our actions around Milligen – why, I will never understand. Jack Leather and his section were very surprised to come under heavy fire from the enemy's light machine guns. No one had expected any action. His section had dug in a defence position around a loading ramp for the barges and inside a hotel. Riflemen Kehoe and Grier and Cpl. H.S. Keeton had their defences in good shape. They were over on the far left. I had just arrived – one of my regular stops to make sure everyone was well dug in, had ammo, food, tea and all those things. In any case, it didn't take much of a skirmish for us to capture eight enemy prisoners.

The prisoners had just been sent back to Nijmegen by boat and, all seeming well, we had just made some tea when the enemy abruptly opened up again. An exploding shell blew me right through the door and down the forty-foot ramp. I landed in one of the old river barges and still had my finger in the ring of the teacup. And the cup wasn't broken!*

My right side was black and blue and it was pretty sore, but I was alive, miraculously, though I had to use a broom handle just to move around.

Another time, we got word that in our advance a fifteen-hundred-weight truck had been left under water. The grapevine system reported that ten gallons of rum were still on board. The next day we went out to find the truck. Meagher, Burke, Freelen and myself did the salvage operation. The water was extremely cold. Meagher and I did the diving and brought up all ten of the gallon jugs, one by one.

We had a very good QOR man back at Battalion HQ in Gordon Wice. He was the regimental quartermaster sergeant, the person who plans for, keeps track of and supplies the outfit with all the food, ammunition and so on that's needed. Gord kept a very careful inventory on the liquor supply, so when he got round to sending someone to retrieve the truck and its rum, he couldn't figure out what could have happened.

And nobody, so far as I know, ever told him.

---

* The Martins still have the cup.

The Calcar-Udem Road

Mooshof and Steeg, the Rhineland's Toughest Fighting
February 1945

The enemy's famous Siegfried Line was eventually captured, and in the third week of February 1945 the transportation unit arrived to move us forward for attacks in the Cleve area and on the Calcar-Udem Road. The enemy forces we were going against would be bitter defenders. They were protecting their escape route home, and the bridge that made it possible. We had no idea this would be the most costly and difficult action of A Company's war.

The Essex Scottish was one of the regiments preceding us in this action, and they had taken heavy casualties. They were led by our former major, now a lieutenant-colonel. This was Jack Pangman, who had been commander for A Company when we were still stationed in New Brunswick. Although we'd considered him stand-offish, we'd appreciated him as a disciplined soldier and a good planner.

We were moving forward to the start line when I saw him. He was dirty and gaunt, tears running down his cheeks. It was hard to compare this man with the major I'd once known when he said, "God bless you in this. We took terrible losses and still didn't get the objective." He'd come to realize how war makes us all equal.

He and the survivors in his regiment were moving back; we were moving forward and beginning to get premonitions of how tough this next phase of the war might get. Anyway, Mooshof, Steeg and Kirsel came next.

Mooshof: A Night of Terrible Losses, February 25 and 26, 1945

We moved forward at 03:00 hours. C Company and B Company were to consolidate the start line by 04:00. Then our company would move up on the right, with D Company taking the left. We were up against very well trained paratroop units. They were the best soldiers the enemy had – tough and determined. They made the SS look like rookies. No wonder the Essex Scottish had such a hard time.

This battle was fought at the brigade level. Our particular job was to capture the road junction at a town called Udem. Our regimental jump-off point was northwest of Keppelin. The first objective was the village of Mooshof. D Company moved up with us.

As our A Company men moved up, we took casualties before we even got to the start line – mortars, artillery, 88s and the Moaning Minnies. The darkness made small difference because tracer bullets and the flash of artillery were lighting up the sky.

Those paratroop soldiers well understood their weaponry and the principles of a fixed line of fire, and they had a good defence position in a group of buildings we would have to secure. The cost of this action would come to seventy men. It was a bitter and ferocious fight, the enemy refusing to yield an inch.

We made the start on time at 4 a.m. with 7 Platoon. They had to take a fortified farm building that contained an 88 and several machine guns. The lieutenant was D.D. Chadbolt; the sergeant Joe Meagher; and the lance sergeant Harold Clyne. They had captured the building by about 6 a.m., but the fighting was fierce. The lieutenant was killed and Joe was wounded in the spleen, so Harold took over the platoon. Then on to the next building – another 88, another heavy machine gun.

Harold Clyne, Bill Grier and Charles Nahwegezhik went after this one. They got it at about 7:30 a.m. My good friend Harold was killed and Charles took a serious wound that later would cost his life. When the chance came, I went out to get him. By now it was daylight. Two machine guns were still in action and they

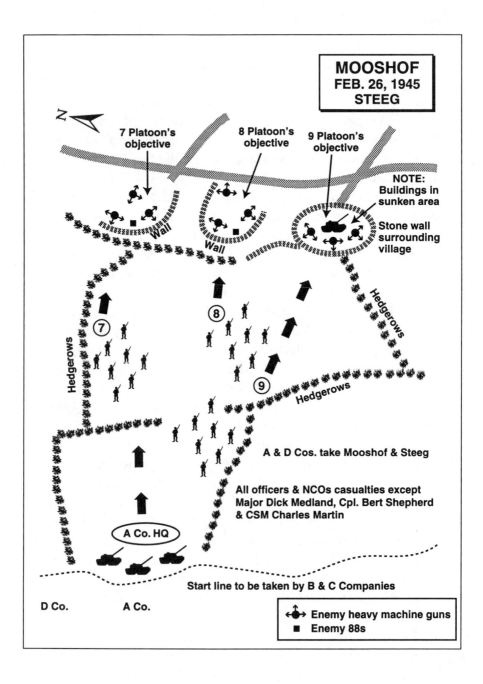

opened up. I got him back but one of their bullets hit Charles in the arm and another grazed my left leg, just enough to draw blood and scare me near to death.

The remnant of the platoon had two-thirds of their objective. We pulled them together and took out the remaining three buildings. It was about nine-thirty in the morning. Objectives achieved, all three of them, but 7 Platoon paid an awful price – their officer killed and all the NCOs dead or wounded.

The battle for these buildings had moved fast. There had been no time to release the livestock. Most of the cows, horses and other livestock were killed or badly shot up.

During one of the split-second frames of tough combat, I heard the breech of an 88 closing. Some of the enemy were just about a hundred feet away and the sounds they made could be recognized. I dove through a door into a litter of half-grown pigs. The shell seemed to follow me, right through the doorway, and most of the pigs were killed. I was underneath, dirty and bloody. But thank goodness it was all pigs' blood.

This was just about the most frightening action of all – knives flashing in the glow of flares, hand-to-hand fighting as artillery bursts light up the sky, death everywhere.

Meanwhile, over on our right flank, 8 Platoon had a similar task as they moved to take out a group of buildings. They took them, but at the same cost as 7 Platoon had paid. Their lieutenant, E.L.N. Grant, was killed just as they reached their first building. Bill Lennox, their sergeant, took over and they got the job finished. But they lost their leaders and were down to half strength. There are no adequate decorations for such men. Their bravery cannot be believed.

Our company HQ was at that point working fine. They had moved up to the area captured by Chadbolt's platoon. The wounded, the ammo supply and the prisoners were all being taken care of, even though all that morning the fire continued to fall on us – artillery and mortars, machine guns, Moaning Minnies, a horrendous and continuous racket of death and destruction.

So now we had two of our objectives, and 9 Platoon made ready to take out the final buildings and complete the job given to us. Again the cost was terrible. Their lieutenant, J.J. Chambers, and his corporal, Bob Dunstan, led the charge for the first group. Chambers was killed. Dunstan was wounded in the arm but still took over the platoon. Their regular sergeant, Jackie Bland, had been LOB on that day and Dunstan, as the next NCO, became the leader.

The last group of buildings we needed had fallen, but at terrible cost. Bert Shepherd moved his section through and consolidated the position. A Company had all its objectives. The survivors were one officer – Dick Medland – and only forty-two other ranks, which included Bert Shepherd and me, the only two of all the NCOs who got through that tough, tough time.

We had been fighting since four in the morning, and now it was nearly noon. We needed to dig in and hold, move out our wounded and gather in our dead. The enemy still put up massive resistance. Our own guns were active. The combined noise level was enormous.

Good old reliable Dick Klintworth brought up the carrier, and the Boss came up in the jeep. We needed these vehicles for our wounded. Klintworth had made sure there was lots of everything we needed – rum, cigarettes, bandages, food and hot, hot tea.

I saw the Boss get on the wireless to report the objective captured and held, but as he spoke the tears were streaming down his face. In the corner our forward observation man, who did the spotting for the artillery, had turned his back but we could hear the racking sobs. People generally are not aware of the extremes of emotion war can produce in the combatants. And that day had been terrible.

Then about that time someone shouted something about a forward slit trench and a wounded soldier. J.A. Riddell and I went out to take a look and we found Al Murray. Al was barely nineteen. When we were digging in on the right flank, he and Rick Brown had made themselves a trench they could be proud of. Still, a sniper had found them and put a bullet in Rick right between the eyes. Then he got Al in the left eye. The bullet had gone right through and out the back of his head. He looked terrible, but his pulse was strong and his colour still good, so first of all we took care of the sniper. We spotted him in a clump of trees about 150 yards off.

No nonsense here. The artillery observer called for a barrage right on the area. To make no mistake about it, the Boss called for the Typhoons to follow up. This was extreme overkill, but we were pretty upset at the time. We would have thrown more at them if we'd had it.

Al weighed about 170. Getting a man of that size out of a five-foot-deep slit trench is not easy. We got him back to the house with the other wounded. Dick Klintworth had already taken the jeep with a load of wounded. All we had left was our Bren carrier to get the remainder out.

Dick Medland was furiously engaged on the communication set, arranging for mortars and artillery. He wanted more Typhoons. Somehow in the midst of all this, I heard him talking to Bert Shepherd – the only unwounded NCO left except for me – about putting together an observation patrol. He was asking Bert to find what was out there.

Shep's classic reply: "What the *?&!@ do you think is out there firing all those machine guns? The *&!@# enemy, of course!"

So we had the carrier and a group of wounded, with critically serious cases in Nahwegezhik and Murray. I explained to the Boss what I wanted to do. It seemed to me I was the only driver available. He said okay, I could go – we had all our extra machine guns well dug in and for the time being they had lots of ammo. I organized the loading. Al and Charles were on stretchers. The other wounded – Bill Lennox, Bob Dunstan, H.S. Keeton, Charles Autonese, Pennell and Les Sheppard – held the stretchers fast.

Bob Dunstan was loud and acting up, creating quite a distraction. He'd been hit in the arm and was now being taken out of action. His greatest wish had been to make sergeant. With all our casualties that probably would have happened. Here he was losing his chance and he sure knew how to grumble.

We had a mile to go to reach the battalion first-aid station, and it was probably the fastest mile that carrier ever travelled. We'd just started when yet another barrage came in – mortars, 75s, 88s and those unbearable Moaning Minnies. Despite their fire and two minefields we made it. Dick Klintworth always said that carrier was never the same afterwards. I said neither was I.

We got out and started unloading the wounded, with one or two of the medical assistants helping. One took a look at Al and said, "Put him over there." He was discounting our man, calculating he had little chance and that others should take priority. He was placing him with the dead.

I told Dunstan, Pennell, Lennox and Sheppard to pick up the stretcher and said, "Follow me." We went into the operating area and they put him on one of the tables. This was messing around in strange territory and they just stood there without saying a word, not even Bill Lennox or Bob Dunstan, and it took a lot to intimidate those two.

They tell me I was covered in blood from head to toe – it was only a short time after the pig episode – and my attitude was far from polite. I don't know all that was said, but I remember saying to Dr. Wayne, "This man still has a good pulse. He needs attention right away."

Wayne stared at me steadily and I don't know what thoughts he might have had. Then he said, "I'll look after him for you." He watched as I went to Al, tears flowing down my face, held his hand and patted his shoulder. "You'll be fine now," I said. "Dr. Wayne has promised to take care of you."*

Well, after that it was back to the group of fortified buildings we'd fought so hard for. Dick Medland was just leaving to go

---

* In 1989 at the forty-fifth D-Day reunion, Charlie saw Al Murray once again. Amazingly Murray remembered it all – the ride, the words and the pat. Al said to Charlie, spacing out his words and giving each one special distinction: "I told my Mom and Dad that it was Company Sergeant-Major Charles Cromwell Martin who saved my life." He repeated this, word for word, many times over the course of the reunion.

back for an O Group at Battalion HQ to finalize the capture of Steeg. Bernie Bruyère and Bert Shepherd were looking after the noon meal (hot), and Parsons and Wilson were guarding twenty prisoners. We were not sending these guys back without an escort because there was one Gestapo officer with them. The Gestapo had orders to shoot any of their men who surrendered.

Then Bernie Bruyère found another Gestapo officer hiding in a cleverly concealed cupboard. We should have been prepared, but it had been a long night and a tough day. We knew that the Gestapo were cruel, ruthless and dedicated to Hitler. As soon as the second Gestapo man came on the scene, the first officer, who had his hands on his head, went for a grandstand play. He pulled a pistol from a hidden holster between his shoulder blades and fired two quick shots at me from ten feet. One drew blood from my right ear; the other went through my camouflage net. Later the boys said that right then you could see the smoke rising and I don't think they meant from the burning headgear.

Two shots from my .38, one in each shoulder. He was lucky I hadn't lost my temper!

The other officer then had to keep his hands straight up. He was stripped to the waist but we found nothing.

For us in A Company the entire action at Mooshof might have been the worst of the war. Others in the battalion also had a bad time. D Company on our left had the other side of Mooshof as one of their objectives. Aubrey Cosens, a sergeant, had his part of a platoon reduced to four and himself. He led a counterattack to take three heavily defended farm buildings. With two tanks, that's exactly what these five surviving soldiers achieved – an example of how ferocious the fighting was everywhere that night. Aubrey was killed by a sniper moments after they'd got the objective. He was awarded the Victoria Cross, the only VC of the war for the Queen's Own, but symbolic we felt of the ferocity of so many actions at so many different points during that battle, some likely simultaneous. No wonder historians so frequently use the word "confused" in trying to describe a night like that.

Steeg: Moving Up with the Wasps, February 26, 1945

When Dick Medland came back from the O Group, he sure wasn't happy. He said we were to attack Steeg. This was maybe a mile or so away, with about a half mile of frontage.

When he arrived, we were having a hot meal and a good shot of rum – courtesy of the salvage job at Waal. In the early afternoon we began to look things over. On the good side, our bad night and tough morning were behind us, we had some rum in our system and a hot meal under our belts. But we now had less than 40 men in what should have been a company fighting strength of maybe 160 or so. It looked tough. Somebody recalled our D-Day axiom: keep going.

We faced a long slope, maybe four to five hundred yards, with unknown guns and mortars waiting for us. The Wasps (flame throwers) wanted to go in with us in our section advance. They said the range was short and they needed to be as close as possible. The sergeant in charge was Wilf Mercer, an old D-Day man from A Company, 7 Platoon. He was keen on doing his very best for us.

Two sections started in the lead. The carriers towing the flame throwers were right with us. Another two sections were behind. Within seconds, the carriers got hits from an 88. At the same time one of them ran over a mine that blew off its track. Wilf was badly wounded. He was trapped and too weak to get out. Two riflemen rushed over to him and I followed, getting a needle of morphine ready.

The riflemen couldn't shake him loose, so I had to give him the needle right through his tunic. All the time he was shouting at us to get away. He knew the flame thrower could go up anytime. Somehow – I don't know how we did it – we yanked him out and managed to get about twenty yards away before, sure enough, up it went, both the unit and the carrier towing it. Not a scrap of metal hit anyone, but the heat was terrific. Our clothes were scorched. It had all taken just a few seconds, or a minute. The stretcher-bearer and three riflemen carried Wilf back to safer ground. His leg was finished but he survived.

The two lead sections started moving again. Then another miracle. White flags appeared everywhere, and over two hundred of their toughest regular army soldiers surrendered. To a battered and shattered under-strength rifle company, the sight of those flags was like rain in the desert. These soldiers who had at last surrendered were well-trained, regular-force men. Many of them were career soldiers. They were, in other words, the very best. We were lucky.

All of us, all four companies in the regiment, had been deep in the same kind of action. At night it's terrifying. You're not sure who's who. We were very fortunate never to have been overrun. A serious counterattack by them on any night or day could have led to disaster for us.

In any case, this one had been one tough, hard, heart-rending battle. We moved on to consolidate and hold at Steeg. The weather was bad. We licked our wounds and dug in.

Further casualties were inflicted on us at Steeg. One of them was accidental. As most of us knew, a Sten gun could do unbelievable things, including going off by itself. This happened with one of our riflemen. The bullet went into his foot. He came limping up to me with tears in his eyes saying it was an accident. Of course it was – that could easily happen. But he was terrified some of us might misinterpret the situation. In the first war a foot wound was the easiest way to get out of the action. This rifleman had been with us since the first wave on June 6. He had been one of our best patrol leaders and he would be badly missed.

Hochwald-Balberger Wald Road

March 2, 1945

The attack on the Hochwald-Balberger Wald was put into operation on March 2. The operation did not go very smoothly for many reasons.

We had two farmhouses about 350 yards away as our target. They were at the south edge of a stand of large, heavy trees. These trees were bigger than normal, so that any possible undergrowth that would give us cover had long since been starved out. Yet they weren't big enough to give us adequate shelter from enemy fire. There were some sunken roads through the woods, but the heavy rains made them no good for tanks or vehicles. There was sort of a main road that looked like it might be worth a try, but again, mud could be a problem – if one vehicle bogged down, the road would be useless to us.

While this was being considered from all angles, I sent back for a hot breakfast. Klintworth and Brough soon returned saying that the road was jammed with traffic and they couldn't get through with the carrier. So this time the three of us headed out on foot, prepared to bring the food back on our backs. We got through, managed to put everything together, and as usual I added a couple of bottles of rum to the pack – no harm in thinking ahead.

I felt sure they'd still be looking at maps and drawing up a battle plan by the time we returned. But it turned out we'd not been long gone when the Boss received a new urgent set of instructions. He was asked to attack the farmhouse at the bottom of the hill immediately. They had realized that Battalion Support and Battalion HQ were in a precarious position, open to artillery, mortar fire and counterattack; the farmhouse had to be taken.

Accordingly, the Boss had sent two platoons of about fifteen men each down the forward slope and through the trees. These woods were full of anti-tank mines and booby traps. Before long they were pinned down by terrific machine-gun fire and were badly exposed to sniper activity.

The Boss, at the start point, stepped on a shoe mine and was badly wounded. The first-aid man got the blood stopped, and as soon as I got back, his tourniquet was the first thing we attended to. Things were now looking pretty grim. The enemy snipers were having a field day. If our two platoons stayed where they were in the woods, they'd be picked off one by one. If they tried dropping back, they'd get the same fate.

I was working my way forward, still with the pack on my back, when I caught a flash and saw a nest of snipers on a platform high in a tree. Very gently I set the pack with the rum in it down for a moment. Then I moved up and took out one of the snipers. I was lucky; I'd spotted him but he'd not seen me. But now we were identified and caught in an ambush. Picking up the rum, I worked my way over to Jackie Bland and suggested we get out of there fast. We would fix swords* and charge straight on.

I turned to Wilson, the Bren-gunner, and said, "Follow me and keep that Bren on automatic." He said, "Charlie, I can't." We were desperate and I flared at him. Then he showed me his right hand. It was shattered. He was a brave guy; he told me if I'd take the Bren, he'd stay with me and carry the extra magazines in his left hand.

In the midst of preparing this crazy charge, we sensibly took time to think about the rum. It was left behind a tree to be picked up later.

We fixed swords, the thirty or forty of us who were left in A Company, and made ready for a head-on straight-ahead charge. It seemed like a movie. We were screaming like Apaches. It really was a do-or-die affair. We couldn't stay and we couldn't go back,

* Other units fix bayonets; the Queen's Own fix swords.

so we went forward. For a time the enemy kept up a steady fire. Then they broke. It was just like one of those films from the first war. They ran, with guns and ammunition boxes if they could. We saw the flashes of enemy uniforms in the gateways or in the broken hedgerow gaps. We took only a few minor casualties; they had many killed and wounded. And we took lots of prisoners. I was never sure, but I think that D Company, who were on our right and were also pinned down, fixed swords on that command from me and went forward at the same time.

I remember rushing one of the two farmhouses. Around the corner an enemy soldier appeared. He was just about as surprised as I was. I took a bayonet wound over my left eye and a bad cut on a finger of my left hand – years later the doctors discovered it had actually been broken – as I tried to ward off his weapon. I fired my Bren at the same time. I had the Bren held with one arm close against my hip. A few rounds went into his left side, wounding him enough to take him out of action.

We got the two farmhouses and found them full of enemy civilians. They were terrified. They believed the savage Canadians would kill them all. I guess our screaming banshee charge hadn't exactly reassured them. That the effect of the charge was so dramatic cannot be explained. For my part, I was screaming on the outside and saying the Lord's Prayer on the inside.*

After we set up our defensive positions and reports were put in, hot food came up and the civilians helped serve the meal. They were very cooperative, but scared. We also found several young soldiers about fourteen or fifteen years of age.

Later that night we went out to have a look at the minefield in front. We succeeded in laying our white tape through it. We expected to use it the next day to push on to the Rhine. But instead we were released from that assignment and moved to a new position in the Reichswald Forest.

---

* It was this action that led to a Military Medal for C.C. Martin.

When our relief came up to take over our position, I carefully explained about the tape and how it marked a safe trail. The tape was ignored. They attacked taking several casualties in that minefield.

For several weeks we reorganized.

We needed major reinforcement and the time to regroup. Our company had lost Dick Medland, our commander, all the platoon commanders and all our NCOs, except Jackie Bland (a sergeant), Bert Shepherd (a corporal) and myself.

Out of over 120 men, we had maybe 40 left. At least a dozen of us wore bandages on wounds considered minor, more or less.

All of us who survived must have been in the protection of God. Every man in that attack deserved the highest award a country can give, and the award they gave me belongs to everyone. The individual gets and wears the medal, but always with the feeling that he's wearing it very much in honour of others who did so much.

Rest Periods
Another Version

During a rest period, the very first thing to do is to provide the company with some sort of sleeping arrangement – a barn, stable, house – whatever can be found. Next, a good hot dinner. Then either sleep or a clean-up, and if the showers are available that's good. All weapons and clothes are checked out, replaced or repaired, and the men catch up on their sleep.

This takes all of the first few days. My version of a rest period isn't quite like others I've been told about, but surely our company could not have been so different. Anyway, as far as I'm concerned, a very important sequence has to be followed.

A soldier can be a very emotional person. He has seen his comrade killed, or badly wounded. It wasn't his fault. He tells himself that. He knew what had to be done. But still he blames himself. He needs to explain how the action went. He needs that burden taken away. Whether it's a company commander or plain Joe rifleman, it's always the same.

What happens is what happens; a soldier needs to come to terms with that.

A lot of this came about perhaps because of one characteristic the Canadian rifleman had in common with all his comrades: bravery. It went through everyone, right up to company commanders. And often it was not just bravery, it was being too brave. That created an awful load for the soldier who survived to bear. He'd think about the things he's seen, the debts he owes to others, the love for one another, and the question that never gets suppressed: why am I here and he's not?

Letters from home, which would accumulate and be delivered to us during the rest, would always spark conversation.

Soldiers needed to talk about girlfriends, mothers, wives and children. Ollie Burke, who was killed at his gun in the Scheldt, always talked about his brother and family, as did so many others.

Many times a soldier would slip me a letter: mail it if you need to. For some reason the boys seemed to bring their troubles to me. I can't explain why. They relaxed talking their troubles away, and then they'd get on to some poker or dice or some other activity. People think of soldiers in rest areas as having riotous crap games, but many of us would relax more quietly with bridge or a game of hearts.

I guess the trick was to get everyone calmed down. When night after night a soldier has stood in a slit trench watching the imaginary movement of every single stone, stump or dead cow, he can get pretty stressed.

Prayer helped. No matter the specific religion of our comrades, in rest areas they found great comfort with prayer. And in conflict they prayed with all their hearts – including me.

Andrew Mowatt, our padre, was a great comfort. He never really preached a sermon. But he had a special way of making the wounded feel better, and the rest of us too. A sad part of war is that the action continues, the men move on and never get a chance to say goodbye or give a graveside prayer for a comrade who's gone. But we knew we had a padre who would and did speak for all of us.

In one of our rest periods before the Rhine, after Major Hogarth had taken over A Company and Dick Medland had gone off to hospital in Horley, out came an order from our new CO that didn't please me at all. After all the action we'd been through he thought we should have a company parade. The men were ordered to clear an area large enough to accommodate this craziness. I felt it was a lot of unnecessary extra work for a rest period when the men should be given a chance to recover. But they set to it with good will, and not even Jackie Bland or Bert Shepherd beefed about all of this foolishness.

Anyway, when the time came, I called A Company smartly to attention. To my surprise some senior officers appeared. I was called forward. Colonel Steve Lett began reading a citation. It seemed that a Distinguished Conduct Medal was being awarded to somebody called Company Sergeant-Major Charles Cromwell Martin for five months of battle in Normandy, France and Holland.

When I had a moment to read it to myself, I was surprised and pleased to see that our A Company had played (they said) a leading part in all of the Queen's Own engagements. I wore the DCM for all, past and present, in A Company.

Crossing the Rhine

March 28, 1945

We crossed the Rhine just south of Emmerich in Germany. Again, the horrors of war. The city of Emmerich looked like the worst of Caen or London. The roads had disappeared under tons of rubble. People were digging in the debris for food and trying to build shelters.

The Canadians and the QOR would push north to the sea to cut off the enemy's army in Holland. There would be many battles from Deventor to Leeuwarden to Sneek for the next three weeks, until the North Sea was reached on April 18.

The Queen's Own captured Eekhorn Zwaarte Scharr and Hoefken with very few casualties. Zutpen was captured from the east; we had minor casualties. Things were so relatively quiet I could walk openly along the east bank of the Ijsselmeer River. On the west side were the enemy, but they had no weapons and nothing was happening.

The Bridge at Rha and Its Buildings

First War Mud
April 5, 1945

We had a strange and mixed up action trying to capture the small town of Rha near a bridge crossing. The enemy command headquarters for the remaining part of Holland was located at Appledoorn, and the bridge was the approach to the road that led there.

The unusualness of this battle might have been a consequence of the complete changeover of our men and leaders. We had received about thirty reinforcements. With some additional men from the HQ unit we were back to close to seventy men, about twenty to each platoon. But everything was too new, too untried, and this included our new company commander.

Major Hogarth had come to us from one of the headquarters companies. In anti-tanks he'd been a lieutenant, then captain, and he came to us about March 12, 1945, as a major. He was very tall and loomed about thirteen inches over me. It seemed he was intent on taking some of the load, sort of anxious to get some action.

In the absence of a lieutenant, Sgt. Jackie Bland was the 9 Platoon commander. He had two brand-new corporals. 8 Platoon had a new officer, a youngish man straight from Canada, not over twenty-one, and he had two brand-new corporals with him as well. The same situation existed with 7 Platoon, headed by Sgt. A.T. Caverley with two new corporals.

Major Hogarth wasn't the only one who was gung-ho. As the whole enemy front began to fold up as we pressed our advance to the North Sea, everyone was looking for prisoners, and maybe some of those who'd not yet had much action felt they were going to run out of war too soon.

At the same time, from April 1 on, everything with us began to go a little out of whack, mostly – as I said – from the too-rapid and wholesale turnover of officers and NCOs. We were, however, making good progress. We Canadians were driving the enemy further east each day. With the Queen's Own in the lead, our 3rd Division was driving straight through to the North Sea and would get there April 18. The plan was to seal off that zone and prevent the enemy from getting back to their homeland, where of course they'd provide nothing but more trouble for us. They wanted to go west and get home. We pushed them east as we drove to our objective.

The enemy had built an elaborate system of trenches that could also have been tank traps. I believe it went all the way from the south of Holland to the North Sea. In our section it paralleled the river and sort of bellied out towards us. Behind it were the buildings and the bridge we would need to go after.

The trenches were very similar to the deep trenches used in the first war, both in the way they were constructed and in the nature of the soil. They were approximately ten or fifteen feet across at the top and three or four feet at the bottom. The soil was heavy clay. Two or three feet of water had collected in them, just enough to make them miserable to be in and most likely of not too much value for any assault.

Our company under Major Hogarth, our new company commander, had captured this little town called Snippeling. We had moved forward to a group of buildings on the outskirts. He called an O Group for the three platoon commanders – the new lieutenant and our two sergeants. The battle plan put forward was not a good one, particularly because the leaders all lacked experience and this plan put them on their own initiative. In fact, it came right out of the old 1940 manual, where the teaching – especially at regimental and brigade levels – was to outflank the enemy. However, since that time we'd learned a lot about ground actions and section jobs. One lesson was that in close actions it was often better to go straight on, using speed and deception, rather than employ the grander designs of flanking and the pin-cer movement, which are sounder if you've got a regiment or two at hand.

In any case the plan had 8 Platoon going south and 7 Platoon north. The only sensible part of it had Jackie Bland and 9 Platoon holding our centre, ready to advance when the objec-tive was taken. When all this flanking had been done, green and yellow flares would be fired and the assault would commence from two directions, just the way the textbooks have it.

Now we would have simultaneous action in three different places by three different platoons, and one of the forward pla-toons had new men – the young lieutenant and his two corpo-rals. And the other platoon, since Caverley was new and only a sergeant, suddenly had a volunteer officer in our new comman-der, Major Hogarth, going with them.

I wanted to go. But this was vetoed. My job was to be in charge of Company HQ, and to coordinate with Battalion HQ our artillery, mortars and aircraft.

First we saw the new lieutenant go out with his unit.

I can pretty well surmise what happened. He didn't follow the trench system as his counterpart in Major Hogarth would. Maybe there was too much water or the sides were too slippery. It seems a good guess the platoon looked the situation over and, noticing a decent-looking protective hedge on the ground above the trenches, decided to go that way. Their objective was the bridge; Hogarth's was the buildings around the bridge.

In less than an hour, one of their riflemen, named Budyna, came back with a large group of prisoners. I was surprised. Prisoners meant they must have gone on the attack. If they'd been ready to launch their assault, why had they not signalled back to us?

Budyna said there was no attack because they were running into no opposition at all. In fact, things looked so good to them that the officer left a small section at his start line and had gone forward again with his force over the blown bridge, advancing foot by foot along the girders and then on into enemy-held positions. He told us they felt reporting to us directly was better than signalling and that way he could also bring in the prisoners.

I found out later that the platoon commander and his men had advanced much too far into enemy territory. They had become pepped up and over-confident by finding it so easy to advance and take so many prisoners. There had been no resistance at the bridge, which was their first objective. But in pressing on, it had got away from them. They took so many prisoners that it began to seem that they had become prisoners of the prisoners as they advanced farther and farther – without orders or anyone's knowledge – into enemy territory. Later on they were picked up, again in the advance, and returned to A Company, but by that time I was out of it.

On the right flank 7 Platoon with Major Hogarth and Sergeant Caverley went right down the trench, waist deep in water, with the buildings in sight. The enemy fired some bursts towards them, plus some mortars, but they were well protected in that deep, muddy trench.

It was not too long before a wounded rifleman came back. His broken arm and chest wound had not upset him too much. It was the platoon he'd left who were in bad trouble. He said they were all soaking wet and covered in mud and that the water had made their weapons useless. Further, it was probably the case that the trench took them nowhere and that with all the mud and slime it was impossible to get up over the parapets. Then somehow the Major had been hit. He might have insisted on "taking a look" and one or two men could have given him a boost. In action, however, many strange things can happen.

If this wounded soldier was any example, his platoon had to be in real difficulty. His rifle was caked with heavy clay mud. He himself was glue, slime and muck from head to toe.

That's what they call time for review. Half of one of our platoons under a new leader was wandering around enemy territory collecting prisoners and meeting no opposition, and the other platoon was on the objective but was taking fire and was poorly equipped for any more action. Despite all this disorganization, we at least knew where our commander was. I thought someone should go up, find him and get some instruction. I was on the set calling for mortars and artillery, and was told that the Typhoons were ready if we wanted them. Before doing anything I wanted a situation report on 7 Platoon and some word from the Major.

I was just asking Jackie Bland to go up to find out if the wounded soldier's information was correct, and what we should do about it, when my astonished ears heard this shout, "Fix swords! Let's take them out with our bare hands."

I was never sure if it was Caverley or Hogarth. It could have been the sergeant. He'd been with us since the end of Normandy and was very aggressive and tough. In fact, he'd have been better on his own than with a bunch of men to look after. Within seconds we heard an enemy machine-gun barrage open up. Then there was dead silence. Bare hands hadn't been enough.

We got most of them back eventually, with Jackie Bland helping the Major, who had taken a bad wound in the arm. There were about twenty-five out of action because of mud and water, a half-dozen wounded, twelve missing from 7 Platoon, and now no company commander.

The wounded were immediately given morphine, wounds were dressed and tourniquets applied where necessary, and all were evacuated back to First Aid.

Now what should we do? One-half of our 8 Platoon had advanced so far that contact was lost. The other half were out there on the objective. Caverley's remnant platoon after that trench action was in no condition for anything. They'd been mired in mud and water and their weapons were useless. The objective still remained in enemy hands. So we had a puzzle for the one platoon left to us who were still able to fight.

So we got a new battle plan. The observation officer called first for mortar, artillery and Typhoons, as requested by us. We then made preparations to go straight down the road. We had a section from Jackie Bland's 9 Platoon along with Budyna – the only rifleman from 8 Platoon we still had.

We had two carriers, one jeep, the signal set, about eight anti-tank men, with Jackie Bland, Jake Leather, Alex Alexander and W.G. Joslin (sergeants and corporals from D-Day and Normandy), and about seventeen riflemen from 9 Platoon, plus Budyna.

We made up a section under Alex, a corporal, and assigned Budyna and Aussem as point men. We used our well-tried tactics of fire and movement and made the most of every bit of cover we could get from the roadside. It was about midnight by this time. We got first the buildings and then the bridge. Within ten minutes the objective was taken. No casualties.

It was the new battle plan that made the difference – another example both of how dependent we always were on good support and of the effectiveness of going straight on. Whatever we did in action was a risk. Most often these flanking movements for small targets just expose the men for a longer time, increase the casualty rate and cause needless delay for the result you're after.

Elliot Dalton, who had been wounded at Le Mesnil-Patry, had returned as acting CO for the battalion. We were glad to report to him that the objective was taken and secure.

Then we were ordered to drop back to the village; another unit took over our position. For the next twenty-four hours, we must have looked like beaten-up specimens from the War of 1812. Half of the men moved around nude looking for dry clothes. Others wore only blankets. We all helped to clean the rifles and webbing, a big job. And those wonderful cooks prepared hot food.

A Company had finally got its objective in the action, but it was far from how these things should go. It must be remembered that you cannot win if you are dead or wounded. Sure, take chances when necessary. A rifleman is there to be a point man and that's always taking a chance but it's a chance that will conserve the lives of the section. The point is not the place for officers or NCOs – it's not the role for them to play unless all is near lost. Then it's another story.

Officers and NCOs are leaders. That kind of leadership should allow one point man – a rifleman – to do his job. And while he's doing it, the leaders can make plans for and give guidance to the entire unit.

All too often I saw men who were too brave, who took on too much themselves, and it did not always carry the day.

The weather became sunny. We received reinforcements and the platoons were reorganized. The new riflemen would quickly establish a comradeship with one another and with the older hands, and we could prepare to move forward.

We had forty-eight hours for this reorganization.

We were glad to get a new company commander in Maj. J.P. Secord, who had earlier reverted to a lesser rank in order to achieve a command in the Queen's Own Rifles. He was to prove a most capable officer. He, too, used these hours effectively to get to know his new NCOs and riflemen.

The Village of Sneek

The Last Battle
April 16, 1945

There is a special plaque prepared by the people living in the village of Sneek to honour the brave men who died there. It says:

If I lose my life — I save it.
1945

The main battle for our company in this area was to close off a causeway and thus stop the enemy retreat out of Holland. The territory was open fields, small farms, small villages and dikes. The only way to go was straight along the dike, which was about thirty feet high. The width across the top was thirty feet or so, which consisted of a sixteen-foot roadway and eight-foot shoulders. Ditches at the bottom collected water, and along the sides of both ditches there were stands of poplars.

Ahead of us was an old stone bridge about twenty feet wide. Hitler Jugend soldiers were nested in a collection of buildings. They had machine guns and mortars, along with ack-ack guns arranged to fire at ground level right down the dike.

Our battle plan put 8 Platoon on the left side. This meant moving along the ditch at the bottom of the dike, waist high in water. They had the rows of poplars on their left. On the right, 9 did the same thing, with a covering line of trees on their right. We had as our support a flame thrower and the Bren carrier.

We were advancing. Machine-gun fire was heavy but we avoided it; it was more or less a harassment. I was alone on the top of the dike. I'd developed a bad chest cold and wanted to avoid that water. And somewhere I'd liberated a piece of heavy

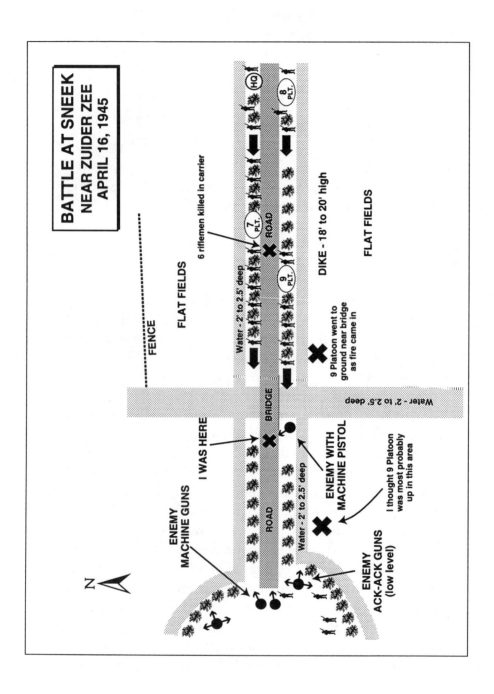

red flannel; I had that stuffed inside for extra warmth. But I was more or less safely located about seventy yards behind 8 Platoon. On my right side, below in the ditch, were the men of 9 Platoon. I was keeping an eye on their progress and staying close.

The flame thrower went rushing up to the small bridge and opened fire, not too effectively. In their enthusiasm they might have created a bit of a problem for the men on the left. This caused them to go to ground. Their area was out of my view but I pieced this together afterwards. Then the Wasp wheeled around and took off, naturally enough since they'd fired everything they had.

They knew at HQ we were operating under strength and the next bit of support they sent up was a Bren-gun carrier and six men. This support was led by one of our Normandy veterans, Cpl. H. Cockburn. He came roaring down the road at top speed with his gun blazing. Those Hitler boys opened fire with the ack-ack guns. Within seconds the carrier was hit and Cockburn, F.R. Shepherd, W.J. Jackson, H.W. White, B.B. Pennell and G.W. Ouderkirk were killed.

The battle went on. I kept moving forward, keeping my eye on the men of 9 Platoon just behind and below me – about a dozen or more, two point men in the lead. While the flame thrower was in action and the carrier was attracting all that fire, the men on the left had sensibly stopped and taken cover. But we didn't know that. We had continued our forward movement. Now, in effect, I had become the point man without realizing it. The only heavy fire from the ack-ack guns had been directed at the carrier and our 8 Platoon. And right after that, the order had gone out for mortars and artillery to drop on them. So I wasn't overly concerned about these kids and their ack-ack and machine guns. Our support people had taken care of them, and the guys in 8 Platoon were up there to occupy them – or so I thought.

Still, when I got to the bridge I was careful, watchful for both mines and enemy signs. On the side there was a stone wall. Three steps past it I sensed a slight movement. To my left a soldier was pointing a Schmeisser at me. It's kind of an automatic pistol with twenty-eight shots in the magazine, a very popular small arms weapon. He let go. Dum-dum bullets ripped me up the right leg and left arm, hit my binoculars and smashed them. At the same instant the ack-ack opened up with shells landing behind me on the bridge. As usual my .38 was tucked in front of my belt. All in the same instant, without drawing, I fired one shot from the waist. The soldier took the bullet above the bridge of his nose just as I was going down. Shrapnel and bits of brick and stone were flying all over. Even today, fifty years later, from time to time fine pieces will work their way out of my ears and back.

Slim Cole, our stretcher-bearer, came running up. All Slim could see was my chest where the main impact of the bullets had hit. A large part of my tunic had just been shot to ribbons. My binoculars were in pieces. The red flannel was ripped into shreds, making it look even more like one bloody mess.

I was partly in shock. Weeping, Slim gave me morphine as I said, "Please let me die in peace." Then I asked for a drink. He pulled out his water bottle. I took a good swig. It was straight rum. I'd always known there was a lot of good in Newfoundlanders.

As all of this was happening, 7 Platoon came up from the rear. Major Secord was in the lead. They took the objective within minutes as the white flags appeared. The battle was over. We had six dead from the carrier action. There were other casualties, of course. But had it not been for the carrier, we could have said this was another objective achieved without loss of life.

The jeep came up. Cole was still crying as they loaded me onto a stretcher. From all the sadness apparent, I felt sure this was it. Major Secord took time to hold me. I remember him saying to me, "Thanks Charlie – for everything."

They rushed me to the first-aid station. Everyone was ready. They tried to cheer me up as they stripped off my clothes and got to work. By now the morphine was working. The doctor moved very quickly to staunch the flow of blood.

Padre Mowatt was there. I was passing out and in but remember seeing the tears flowing down his face, and thinking to myself, this is it – if he's crying like that I'm a goner.

I remember a truck ambulance. They loaded me onto it, to get me back to a base hospital. The ambulance was in a hurry and ran off the road into a ditch. Eventually they got themselves towed out but not without a few jerks and bumps which didn't help. We arrived at the hospital. My leg wounds had started to bleed heavily, so they put the stretcher on the floor near the entrance where the blood wouldn't cause too much damage. Luckily a young nurse happened to see this spreading pool of blood on the floor. I barely remember her calling for help.

The surgeon rushed me into the operating room to remove the bullets. Then, as best he could, he got the bone parts back together and reattached the nerves.

When he was working on my arm, I came to for a few seconds, looked down at what he was doing and said, "Don't take it off!" I remember the doctor shouting "More ether!" Then I passed out for good. For me that day, April 16, 1945, was the end of the war.

I did not recover consciousness until May 8. A pretty nurse was sitting beside me. Winston Churchill was announcing over the hospital radio system that the war was over.

The nurse asked me if I was hungry. What would I like to eat?

"Poached eggs on toast. Six please."

I ate one and threw up.

My main concern was how to get in touch with Vi. I spoke to a visitor and asked him to send a telegram. In the meantime, Vi had received a letter from Padre Mowatt telling her I had been wounded. To make it easier for her, he had written "slightly wounded."

Vi didn't get my wire till May 10. Even then it didn't help her much, since under wartime conditions the telegraph office could not reveal the place of origin. Victory in Europe didn't change the fact that there was still fighting in the South Pacific.

I finally got a letter to her identifying my hospital. She arrived! I was wobbly on my crutches and couldn't contain my excitement. I very nearly knocked her over.

After we settled down from our embrace and all the things people blurt out at such a time, she took a careful look at me. My right hip, stomach and chest were in a cast. My left arm was in a cast. I'd lost a tremendous amount of weight.

She said, "If this is slightly wounded, I'd hate to see the major ones."

It was August before they sent me home, still on crutches, on the hospital ship *Letitia*.

Vi was still in the army; she followed later. There was a whole new world to be faced by riflemen and hundreds of thousands of others. We had fought to preserve one world; now, in 1945 we faced another.

But as everyone knows, that's another story.

Epilogue

It's true, what some are surely thinking: what a horrible price to pay. If this is what war is, then never again. None could say it any stronger than we. We said it then and we say it today.

But it was a time when cruelty and tyranny were rampant pretty well throughout the world. We fought to stop it. We fought for freedom then, and for the freedom we have today. And we knew right from the start it would not be easy and it would not be pretty.

But we were nonetheless hungry and impatient for June 6, 1944, because it was the long-awaited climax of many battles and trials by many soldiers and civilians in many places.

We were sensitive about Dunkirk. Our people in 1940 had already landed in France; those who got back were lucky. We knew all about the Battle of Britain and the defence of London. Both the Middle and Far East had a significant place in the war, and we well understood the effort being made across the world in so many different theatres and actions.

Our planners had learned from the slaughter at Dieppe, two years before. This time we had complete naval and artillery support. And our air power had significantly advanced. The tactical lessons hard-learned on August 19, 1942, saved lives on June 6, 1944.

And in 1943, another combined force of Canadian, British, Indian – including turbaned Sikhs – and Americans had succeeded in making the beginnings of a foothold in Europe. The Italian campaign started with the Sicily invasion in July. Canadian soldiers with their allies held down some of the very best enemy troops along with many of their top generals.

If these well-trained and combat-experienced enemy forces had been available to face the Allies in Normandy during June of

1944, our invasion would have been more costly by far. The enemy in fact would have had a very good chance during those first four weeks of breaking through the Allied defence. Even the beachhead itself might have been a disaster. All of that we know now; in 1944 all we had were intelligence reports, theories, hopes, fears and a lot of determination to get a job done.

Our people believed in this country, were proud to be known as Canadians, and loved their way of life, family, religion and freedom.

Pride and love for the regiment became embedded. Risking life time and time again for your comrades became a daily and even hourly routine.

Every soldier from rifleman to top command did the job – to the best of his ability and often, miraculously, way beyond. And from Bernières-sur-Mer in June through to Falaise in August, and then on to the North Sea in Holland and to Germany, no soldier ever said no to any request from me. The word no was not a part of our vocabulary. Not in B, C or D companies, and especially not in A Company and its three platoons.

I can't forget what these men achieved. The cost, the numbers – certainly that's frightful to think about. But all of us knew it had to be done. And the real price is known only to those spared. We remember always the bravery and devotion of those who stayed behind. They are comrades forever young and locked in memory – still devoted, still loving, still proud.

They are riflemen forever.

"CC"
March 1994

Acknowledgments

These stories and these people were rising like corks in a sea of suppressed memory. I wanted to tell the tale. Yet I really had no notion of how to go about it.

My special thanks to Roy Whitsed, who became my editor and other voice. His gently probing questions transformed fragments of memory into words, and always he seemed able to get the words into text and in the proper order – not always an easy thing, when I was recalling combat that proceeded on two or three flanks. Marlene Klopfer was my first editor and transcriber. I think one day she just gave up and found Roy, but she remained to supervise the manuscript and she continuously watched over the corrections and amendments. And a thank you to Carolyn Hruska, along with thanks to her earlier counterparts, for the keyboard work done over almost two years (since April 1991), week after week, as memory flowed, add-ons increased and the story developed.

My appreciation too to all the people at Dundurn Press, particularly Judith Turnbull, the editor; Andy Tong, the book's designer; and Kirk Howard, the press's president, who made the decision to go ahead. I also want to mention the warm support of Dundurn's Nadine Stoikoff and Jeanne MacDonald.

And last of all and most of all, I thank Vi, my beautiful war bride, who gave me so much encouragement and understanding over the many months this book absorbed so much of my thought and attention.

APPENDIX A
LETTERS

FROM DICK "THE BOSS" MEDLAND
" … to give and carry out his orders so as to ensure the greatest comfort and safety of his men."

Major R. A. Medland
2nd Can Gen Hosp.
Horley
Surrey
England.
23 Mar. 45.

Dear Charles,

Thanks ever so much for your letter. It was bloody good to hear from you. Also got the battle dress in good shape plus the news of your D.C.M. Charlie if you got the V.C and a thousand other gongs it still would not be sufficient reward. But anyway the D.C.M. is a small reminder of what I, and many others, think of you.

Hospital life is slightly slow but comes as a welcome rest. And although I miss you fellows

2

more than I can tell – I still feel that the rest will do me good. I had no idea I was so tired. The food is top-hole here, as are the nursing sisters. So all in all I'm not suffering.

Today, for the first time, I got out in the sunshine, with the aid of crutches and my walking stick. Already I am known in this area for my walking stick. My fame is spreading!

Young McLean (remember) was in to see me today. He is doing well and will be back in a month or so. He was quite cut-up about young Wilson being killed. Also Lance Riggs & Auld were in. Auld goes back to Canada as a

3. Captain instructor [redacted] 3/ [redacted]

[redacted]

[redacted]

Had a letter from Capt. Pond and he seems to think the new set-up is pretty good. I hope the feeling is general. Charlie it is absolutely essential that maj. Hogarth gets the same cooperation and assistance that I got. You, as you know, are the man that can influence the greatest amount of men on any subject. One thing that should be the banner line of A Coy is the motto "The time to back me up is when you think I'm wrong" If they all follow that princi

4.

There will be few heart breaks and many successes.

On Sunday next I will know more or less definitely whether the foot is going to be any good again or not. I'll let you know as soon as I can. I've got my fingers crossed, because I really want to get back with you – and soon too!!

Give my best to all the gang and tell them to write. If Rhn Smith (Sigs) is still with you tell him to write too will you. So until next time

yours as ever
The Boss.

A Coy.   Major A. D. Midland
1st Queens Own Rifles of Canada.   24 Cdn. Gen. Hosp.
                         Horley
                         Surrey
                         17 Apr. 45.

My Dear Charles,

It is so darn hot here today that I can hardly breath. The weather reminds me of those long, hot days when we raced across France in the wake of the great German Army. Only, here are none of the clouds of dust - the stink of dead flesh, or the excitement of a victorious march. Everything is quiet - nature is settling in its Summer locale, as the trees become festive in their first bashful green. One can find peace and solace in the quiet of the English Spring - but oh Charlie there is so much missing.

In my younger days, I often worked out jig-saw puzzles. At one time I was pretty good. Now ⅔ I find myself in the midst of the biggest puzzle of my life. It is a puzzle of the mind - but no less difficult because of it. There are some pieces missing though Charlie. Pieces which are "somewhere in Europe".

It ludicrous, what my mind has been doing lately. Scheming this way and that, only to know at the outset that all the scheming of ~~my~~ an even more fertile brain than mine, could not finish the puzzle without the pieces. But this awful idleness - this emptiness of purpose and life is driving me crazy. And for it, I feel humble and disgusted. For how much better, luckier is my life now, than it was. True I was with friends, but as far as security went. there was none. And my only answer is that I would forgo the security

and the comfort of this 3/. life in England - to
be with my men - my best friends - for in
them lies my purpose in life - my love
and it is my firm desire to extend my
total energy towards making their lives,
happy, useful and full. But what happens.
I am lying here - useless to man and
beast. My job was left unfinished and
I am now incapable of finishing it.

As time goes on C.C., my heart
grows heavy. Time in its inexpendable
supplies lies heavy on my hands and
the continuous thoughts which run thru
my mind are of nothing but you chaps.

But all this chatter can be of
little interest to you, who have so much
to do. You who value life more than any
because of the very indefinite nature of
it; you who love as no one else can

in order to get your full measure of it;
I have no right to even appear unhappy.
But I do, Charlie. I do to you because
I know you will understand.

I will never forget that church service
we had on 25 Feb. That was just before
our push when we lost Punchy Patterson and
all the others. And that night when I got the
whole company together. A thrill went right
through me Charlie - I knew - I could feel
the mutual love, trust and respect that was
the spark of life to us all. And now that
my whole being can look back at those
days - those faces - I can realize as I never
did how good God has been to me. This
may sound like the last will and testament
of a dying man. It is far from it. Instead
it the documentary expression of one small.
unimportant human being, whose eyes
have become clear to bravery and devotion

which we so tersely call "duty". Wealthy indeed, is the man who can call all those men his friends. I never talked much about these things Charlie, but it may now be an inspiration to those who are left; those who remember me, to know how I have always felt.

It is the sacred duty of every commander, to ensure that his orders are given and carried out so as to bring complete and absolute destruction to the forces of evil. But, and I emphasize this, it is also his most sacred duty to give and carry out his orders so as to ensure the greatest comfort and safety of his men. A commander works for his men, not vice versa.

Enough for now Charlie. I am always thinking of you. Soon I'll be back I hope. My best to all.

Always your
Boss.

FROM ANDREW MOWATT, CHAPLAIN, THE QUEEN'S OWN RIFLES

Queen's Own Rifles of Canada,
S.E.O., 17th April 45.

Dear Mrs. Martin,

By now you will have heard that Charlie was slightly wounded the day before yesterday. Believe it or not, we were all really glad as it will give him a well-deserved rest. He has been working like a Trojan for a long time now and had done a wonderful piece of work.

I can't tell you how much he has inspired us all by his devotion to duty and care for his men. We were thrilled when he was awarded the D.C.M. although we all felt he deserved an even higher award — although the D.C.M. is very high too. Our artillery officer here, Major Lawson, told me that Charlie deserves the V.C. A few days ago one of the boys told me that it did him a world of good just to see Charlie; now.

He is absolutely fearless in battle. Charlie has a very strong faith and it certainly has brought him through. He has probably had more close shaves than anyone in The Queen's Own. That is one reason why we are glad that he received the wounds (one in leg and one in arm) which are not at all serious and yet enough to give him a rest and keep him out of danger.

You may have heard from him before you do even this. In any case, you have no reason to worry about Charlie.

I hope you are keeping well yourself now. The best of everything to you.

Sincerely,

Andrew Mowatt
(Chaplain Q.O.R.)

A. Mowatt

P.S. One big shell fragment cut a big gash in Charlie's tunic, shirt, and underwear and missed him completely. He all feel that God is protecting him.

A.M.

FROM PARENTS WHOSE SONS WERE NOT RETURNING

235 Thompson Drive
Sturgeon Creek
Man.
Canada

Dear Charlie,

May I call you that? or did Jim Bunne call you Chuck as so many get called?

We got your so welcome letter - thank you again and again because it told us what we wanted to know that Jim died nd suffer and that he had a decent burial in the Division Cemetery. That means we shall be told the number of his grave & he'll have a cross with his name on.

He must have asked you to write for yours is the only one coming to the home address, all else has gone to my husband's office - the address Jim gave. I guess he wanted to save me the shock. And it was. it was just as much shock to hear it over the phone. I wonder if you would write again Charlie

2) and let us have some more news about Jim. What was it he did on to-day that the Toronto paper called him a hero. Mei? We shall never know unless someone tells us. We know that the Ft Garry tanks from Winnipeg had a job to land owing to the heavy seas. Ask the officer who censors the mail if you could give us a few details. - We would be so very grateful for them.

I have a notion Jim helped you out in some fashion - you say he was like a father to you - that's like his Dad always helping quietly. Yes, he was hare and cow alright and well loved everywhere.

Another thing - could you tell me if there were any groups taken - photos I mean - are you in that group the Irvington Platoon group taken at Camp Borden July/43?

I am so hoping to hear again + all will write to you - anything you can remember to tell us - we shall treasure it.

Goodbye Charlie - you don't put your rank so don't be offended if I put Rifleman. All good wishes to you and thanks again.   Sincerely yours Jessie Browne
Jim's Mum.   (Mrs E. W. Browne)

Sept. 15/44

Dear Charlie

just a line from Gerry's Dad
I want to thank you very
much for dropping us a
line. we miss Gerry's letters
very much. their are lots
of things I would love to
ask you but I know you
cannot tell me. but I
hope & Pray some day
we can meet. I have a
Brother some where in France
you might run across him
I will send you his adress

11

Please write us again
& tell us all you can &
when you come back
drop us a line & we will
go to see you or you
come & make us a visit
Good Luck & God
Bless you

C-51266 Bdr. Winter Tom
34 Bty 14 Cdn. Fd. Regt. R.C.A.
C.A.O

this is Gerry's uncles address he
wrote to Gerry different times but they
didn't see each other they weren't
far apart he would be glad to hear from
you. Winters you.

Hampton, Ont. Sept. 14.

Dear Charlee,-

Received your letter to-day & you will never know how much that letter means to my husband & myself—we had so hoped & prayed that someone would send us some information or details about our dear son. And in this message I wish to thank you from the bottom of my heart for your kindness & thoughtfulness to us. No words can express how we felt & how much we really miss Gerry. But I was glad to hear he did not suffer & that he was buried in a

2

cemetry. I take from what you said you were with him & in the same unit so I am sending this to the A O R hoping you get it O.K & I am wishing you the best of luck & would like to keep in touch with you would you mind telling me where you live I know quite a few Martins you might be one of their sons I sent Gerry some boxes I don't think he would of received them all & I didn't have any other address on them I would be more than pleased if their were any way for you to get them I don't know what

3

they do with their parcels. If I
could write to them I would
do so I know Guy would
want you or someone who knew
them to get them & so would I.
Guy also had quite a few
personal belongings I would
love to have did he have
them on him when you saw
him. I was talking to a chap
that was wounded in Italy
& he said quite often their
watches & etc are stolen.
How long had you known Guy
& been with him. It all seems
so short since he went away

he didn't loose much time just
pushed a head 9 months & 17 days
from the day he enlisted to Aug
12. we received the telegram Aug 19.
This is not an easy thing to answer
your letter I feel so sad & lonely I
hope you will understand & I
know it wasn't easy for you
to write us perhaps we will
meet some day when this terrible
war is over I would like to
send you a box or something I
feel so thankful to you I
will close hoping to hear from
you again. I remain
               Guy's Mother.
Mrs Violet Winter
King St.   Hamilton, Ont. Can.

Mr Charles A Martin   September 19th/44

Mrs Willis & I thank you so much
also all the boys of A Coy. for your
very kind thoughts expressed in
your letter which we received
on the 18th it is grand to know.
Our son had the esteem & con-
fidence of all his buddies as
he seems to be so well liked & we
know. he has at all times tried
to please others during his life
even at the cost of his own Comfort.
also we are proud to hear of him
as being everything a man could
be especially while taking part
in this war. & of Course we who
are too old for this war as
soldiers know from the experience
we had in the last one, that
any fellow who has freely offered
his services in this one is every
inch a man. yes we are proud

2

of every one of you we know you
will carry on and finish the
job. Start making special
efforts to make up for the loss of those
taken away even in the midst
of life so God bless you Charles
and also the others of A Coy etc
I am sure have used you as their
spokesman being I presume his
most close friend in the service
and we pray that this conflict
which is taking place to free the
world of a fanatical fancy of a super
Man race of people called Nazis
~~may soon be over~~ ~~finishing when~~
be home again to live in peace
with us if ever you come out our
way when in the West end of Toronto
that you will call on us in Mt
Dennis we do not live in a mansion
and any friend of Clyds is always
welcome once again we thank

you for your kind thoughts & 3
expression of sympathy we thank
God that our Son lived a good
clean life and did what he
could which is the highest
& most honourable service one
Man can do for during a lifetime
giving his life as many thousands
of others have done during this war
that those who are left might be
free. It is a sad blow to his Mother
& I but we have the knowledge that
where God lays the hand of death
upon us we realize our services on
earth are finished & one is not
lost is not but just gone before to
await the time when those who
are left to carry on shall receive
the "well done" enter into the joy
of the Lord. O God bless & keep you
& your & his friends bringing a
speedy end & as speedy a return

home as possible — thanking you & your
brothers in arms once again for
your kindness & thoughtfulness at
this time.

      Respectfully Yours

      J.R. & Mrs. Willis

      Sydney's Mother & Dad

      J.R. Willis
      60 Humber Blvd
      Mt Dennis
      Toronto 9.

Your letter was
addressed to our oldest son's home

APPENDIX B
THE BIG TWO BUGLE
NEWSLETTER OF THE QUEEN'S OWN

EDITOR
Sjt S D WATSON

A/EDITOR AND ARTIST
Cpl A IRVINE

No 24   Vol III

D plus 174   GERMANY   27 Nov 44

EDITORIAL

As you will see upon perusal of the following page we have persuaded Major H E DALTON, Mk II, to climb out of his custom built slit trench long enough to dash off a short literary effort for the benefit of you water-logged would be Dutchmen. After reading the original manuscript it was pointed out to us that it would probably set our circulation figures back by at least six months, but being gambling men at heart we're taking that chance. Who knows we might have unearthed a second Stephen Leacock! Many thanks, sir, we hope that you have time, between fulfilling the obligations, to come around again soon.

To "A" Coy we extend our thanks for their flight into the future, and might say that we are looking forward to the next "vision".

It has also been drawn to our attention that the Editors of this journal committed the grave error last issue by stating that the "Bugle" was published in HOLLAND, knowing full well that it should have borne the heading "published in GERMANY". This was quite true, but after nearly five years of Security lectures from all personnel, from Pl Sjt to GOC we have finally taken these little points to heart.

The "Bugle" would like to take this opportunity of extending congratulations to all ranks for the good work that has helped to make our present position possible. It gives us great pride to be able to announce that we are the first Canadian Infantry Battalion to set up our HQ within the borders of the Third Reich. Nice going lads!

The Editor

A CHALLENGE FROM MK II

MAJ H.E. DALTON - CVSM AND 1 GOLD BAR

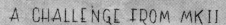

I have been asked by my many creditors in "F" Echelon to write a short note for the Big "2" Bugle, thus informing my creditors in "A" and "B" and sundry echelons that I have returned to the fold.

By submerging myself in water in HOLLAND and hiding in pill-boxes in CALAIS, I have, until now, successfully forestalled the editors of this 'ar chronicle. However, I have decided, having received a ten million mark note from an admirer, that I can now afford to let all and sundry know that I am back and ready to face the financial crisis.

Seriously tho', I'm damned glad to be back again for two reasons. First, as those of you who have been away will agree, if you are going to soldier, the only place to do it is with the old regiment. Secondly, my "Q" matters are solid by the fact that I can now borrow from my brother with no thought of ever signing a document or returning same.

To finish this enlightening note. As you all probably know, I have been with every company in the battalion. Each one, I have convinced myself, was better than the previous one. I am not putting myself out on a limb by making any rash statements but if any company would like to take on my present company at baseball, soccer, shooting, crap, marching, running, "I" Tests, "Q" Tests, darts, knock-rummy and OTHER indoor sports, please see my CSM who will arrange the whole thing (including the financial side.) Any drinking contests will be looked after by the Company Commander himself!

Best of luck to you all.

Commanding "B" Company
1 Bn The Q O R of C

A SHORT SHORT STORY

One morning recently, a young woman
Got out of bed
Slipped into her slippers,
Raised the shade,
Uncovered the parrot,
Put on the coffee pot,
Answered the phone,
And heard a masculine voice say:
"Hello Honey, I have just got off the ship
and have 24 hours leave, I am coming
right up"
So the lady unlocked the door,
Took off the coffee pot,
Pulled down the shade,
Covered the parrot,
Slipped out of her slippers,
Slipped into bed,
And heard the parrot mumble,
"Jeepers, what a short day!"

CHRYSTAL GAZING
WITH A COY

Among one of our many prized possessions - loot to those whose standard of living is low - is a most magnificent chrystal! It is of pocket size and awfully, awfully round: but let not its minute size bring thoughts of impotence, for this chrystal has provided some very happy times and given us a keen insight into the future. As a matter of fact it is felt by the experts, of whom we appear to have many, that very shortly the use of "Shelreps" and "Moreps" will be stodgy and old fashioned. For with our little chrystal we will be able to, not only tell from where sprang the .88 but also - and this is much more important- when they're coming.

However, we see enough of war - so our main interest is wrapped up in the future. After all our past is known to us and we feel that the less it is known to others - the better! As a consequence let us tell of one or two of our more interesting visions.

Our first experience presented a most starting vision, one we had not seen for some time. There in the bold half light of a sinking St. CATHARINES sun was our friend. He appeared to be unemployed. His once tailored suit was now showing the signs of age - but so was he. Our image became faint while a sepulchral voice softly put us in the chronological picture. It was, we learned, after the war. The vision had been discharged (lucky man) and apparently, within the limits of our time-honoured law, had been forced to vacate his park bench. Now that the full resources of the NAAFI were no longer at his disposal, he had found himself in the uncomfortable position of having to find billets. Of course being a former CQMS, this procedure was unknown to the vision.

The chrystal then gave forth once more, and we saw, dimly now for the sun had set, and the St CATHARINES Curfew had come into effect. To continue, after calling on his former Company Commander, who referred him to his former Second-in-Command, who referred him to the former RQMS, who asked him why the hell he would wake a guy up with such a foolish question, the vision recalled with a sigh of remorse, that now all he had left to do was call on his former storeman. After all, his former storeman used to do all the work anyway. However, this also failed (perhaps the chrystal will tell us where the former storeman was - but not just now.) All angles tried and retried, the vision slipped slowly and silently, sniping buts as he went, back to his favorite park-bench. As the vision fades in a mumble-jumble of NAAFI girls, irate RQMS's and boots, ankle high, we see him drifting off into the arms of mighty Morpheus - a condition which renders him most recognizable to his old friends!

ooOoo

MY BEST GAL

Of a girl each guy has a dream
Perhaps she's dark or maybe fair,
With skin like honeyed cream
And golden flaming hair.

With eyes of hazel, brown or blue
A heart as pure as gold
To only you she is true
A lover, staunch and old.

One who waits for your return
And counts each passing day,
Those eyes will flash and burn
When you pass her way.

That girl waits for me
With my father and my brother,
In that land across the sea
Yes, that girl is my mother.
                        Duff/

OFF THE RECORD

MOE: "Why do rabbits have more fun than people?"
GUS: "Because there's so many more rabbits than people."
MOE: "Why are there so many more rabbits than people?"
GUS: "Because rabbits have more fun than people?"
                        from "D" Coy.

ooOoo

CSM Martin came back to billets with a German helmet slung over his shoulder.
"I had to kill a hundred Germans for this," he announced.
"Why?" asked Sjt Lennox.
"Had to get the right size." said the CSM.

THE WALKING DEAD

Many suggestions have been put forth during the past four years on how to avert all future wars. To-date, the most logical plan has been originated by a local newspaper from home. They suggest that, upon the cessation of hostilities, Canada's pride and joy, the "Zombie" Army, for the past few years reposing in the wilds of Toronto, Montreal and Vancouver, should be shipped lock, stock and barrel to the Reich. There they would be quite only ~~~~~~ in the ~~~~ ~~~~~. In this manner, the peace and safety of the world would be assured, for, as everyone is well aware - the male progeny of the Zombie will never fight!

KORN FROM CUFF

We have a Capt Dunkelman,
Who's Morters beat the band,
A Cherubic bunch of cheer and joy-
The Rogue of No Man's Land;

He creaks up to his O-Pip
With his morters ably manned,
And gives out humnier orders -
This Rogue of No Man's Land;

When he gets back home again
He'll drink beer, bottled and canned,
And we will drink a healthy toast -
To the Rogue of No Man's Land!

We have a Mr Pickup
In our Pioneer Platoon,
With a cheery dreamy face
as fresh as a morn in June.

His chatter is so bright,
His corn right off the cob,
But when you badly need him,
He's right there on the job.

You won't know how to take him
When you see him brush and slick-up
But you'll find he's a darned good ~~~~
The same Lieutenant Pickup

Don't back the attack by courting a SWACK,
Or "making the rounds" with a WAVE,
Just lie in your trench - and dream of the wench,
And buy bonds with the money you save!!

HIGHLIGHT OF THE WEEK

Forty (40) 3 Cdn Inf Div men proceed home on leave - 16,000 "Zombies" drafted for overseas service - to fill the gap! Which makes it about ev~

"GOING WEST"

APPENDIX C
SIGNED RECOMMENDATIONS FOR DCM AND MM
AWARDED TO CHARLES CROMWELL MARTIN
WITH LETTERS OF CONGRATULATION

C.F.A. 1
40/F & 6/1420 (3080)

Date recommendation
passed forward

8 Cdn Inf Brigade 3 Cdn Inf Division 2 Cdn Corps

	Received	Passed
Originated	5 Nov 44	
Brigade	5 Nov	6 Nov 44
Division	8 Nov	13 Nov 44
Corps	NOV 1 3	NOV 1 5
Army	7 NOV 1944	2 7 NOV 1944

Schedule No. .... Unit 1st Bn The QOR of C (CIC)
(to be left blank)

Army No. and Rank B63919 W O II (CSM)

Name MARTIN, Charles Cromwell
(Christian names must be stated)

Action for which commended (Date and place of action must be stated)	Recommended by	Honour or Reward	(To be left blank)
B63919 CSM MARTIN, Charles Cromwell landed with the assault coys on D Day and has taken a leading part in all engagements in which this battalion has been committed since that date. He has been subjected to the heaviest shell, mortar and MG fire on many occasions, and at all times his coolness under fire and in actual contact with the enemy has been a source of help and encouragement to the men under his command. He has personally accounted for many enemy casualties both dead and prisoners. His utter disregard for personal safety has upon many occasions been the means of saving lives of many of his men, while his leadership ability has been the means for the success of many actions undertaken by "A" Coy during the past five months. (G G Simonds) Lt-Gen Comd 2 Cdn Corps Nov 44	as-all en-Lt-col S M LETT, (J A ROBERTS) DSO Lt-Col T/Comd 8 Cdn Inf Bde. (D C Spry) Maj-Gen GOC 3 Cdn Inf Div	Distinguished Conduct Medal Periodical Award.	P.T.O.

H. O. C. ....
G.O.C.-in-C.
First Canadian Army

If a casualty as under, fill in date.

Nature of Casualty	Date
Killed in action	
Died of Wounds	
Died	
Missing	
Prisoner of War	

CPA 1
40/P & S/1420 (5918)

8 Cdn Inf Brigade 3 Cdn Inf Division 2 Cdn Inf Corps
1st Bn The Queen's Own
Schedule No. .... Unit Rifles of Canada (CIC)
(to be left blank)

Army No. and Rank B63919 Company Sergeant-Major
(Warrant Officer Class II)
Name MARTIN, Charles Cromwell D.C.M.
(Christian names must be stated)

Date recommendation passed forward		
	Received	Passed
Brigade	8 Mar	8 Mar 45
Division	19 Mar	19 Apr 45
Corps	APR 25 5 MAY 1945	MAY 4
Army		11 MAY 1945

Action for which commended (Date and place of action must be stated)	Recommended by	Honour or Reward	(To be left blank)
	(SM LETT) Lt-col DSO	Bar to the M.M.	Military Medal 1945
	Jas A Roberts (J.A. Roberts) Brig Comd 8 Cdn Inf Bde		
	(RH Keefler) Maj-Gen GOC 3 Cdn Inf Div		
	(G.G. Simonds) Lt Gen Comd 2 Cdn Corps 30. Apr 45		
	(Crerar) Gen. G.O.C.-in-C. First Canadian Army.		PTO

On the morning of 4 March 1945, "A" Company, 1st Bn The Queen's Own Rifles of Canada was committed to an attack on BALBERGER WALD at the southern end of the HOCHWALD FOREST. In the initial stage of the attack and unbeknown to the platoon commanders ahead, the company commander of "A" Company was severly wounded. The fighting at this particular time was confused and due to the denseness of the woods, control was difficult to maintain.

CSM MARTIN of "A" Company, picked up a Bren gun and made his way under intense enemy fire to the right flank of the company. Upon reaching the right flank, CSM MARTIN personally led the attack of his men in a daring charge at the enemy. Firing the Bren Gun from the hip and constantly urging the men on, B63919 Charles Cromwell MARTIN he inspired the men to great heights. The enemy were completely routed and left behind 26 dead and 47 prisoners. CSM MARTIN personally accounted

(2)

B63919 Company Sergeant-Major Charles Cromwell MARTIN

for 11 enemy dead.

This magnificent example of courage, coolness in action, ability to inspire men, and devotion to duty on the part of CSM MARTIN was mainly responsible for the success of "A" Company, 1st Bn The Queen's Own Rifles of Canada, in this attack.

B. L. Montgomery

FIELD MARSHAL
COMMANDER-IN-CHIEF
21 ARMY GROUP.

If a casualty as under, fill in date

Nature of Casualty	Date
Killed in action	
Died of Wounds	
Died	
Missing	
Prisoner of War	

HEADQUARTERS
THIRD CANADIAN INFANTRY DIVISION

Office of the GOC

23 May 45

Dear Martin -

I congratulate you upon the award
of the Military Medal and for the gallant
and distinguished services you have
rendered.

Major-General
GOC 3 Cdn Inf Div

B 63919 WO II (CSM) CC Martin, DCM MM
QOR of C

1st Battalion

The Queen's Own Rifles of Canada

Holland   31 May 45

CSM Martin, CC   DCM, MM
9 Cdn Gen Hospital
Cdn Army, England

Dear CSM Martin:

I extend to you, on behalf of all members
of the regiment, our congratulations on the
award of the Military Medal for your very gallant and extremely meritorious services, rendered
to this battalion upon more than one occasion.

We are all very happy that you have received
this, and I personally, am waiting to hear you
make another one of your famous speeches in the
Sargeant's mess.

I hope that you are beginning to grow all
together again, and that it will not be long
before we see you again.

sincerely

(S M LETT)   Lt.-col
Comd 1 Bn The Q O R of C (AF)

SML/w

OFFICE OF THE
ADJUTANT-GENERAL

H.Q. 405-M-46545
(D.R. 3)

DEPARTMENT OF NATIONAL DEFENCE
ARMY

CANADA

Ottawa, Ontario,

June 29th, 1945.

Mrs. Violet Martin,
16 Marx Tice,
Chopwell, Newcastle,
England.

Dear Mrs. Martin:-

It is with much pleasure that I write you
on behalf of the Minister of National Defence and
Members of the Army Council to congratulate you and
the members of your family on the honour and distinction which has come to your husband, Company
Sergeant-Major Charles Cromwell Martin, DCM, through
the award to him of the Military Medal, in recognition
of gallant and distinguished conduct in the field.

Yours sincerely,

(A.E. Walford),
Major-General,
Adjutant-General.

APPENDIX D
HONOURS AWARDED TO MEMBERS OF A COMPANY, THE QUEEN'S OWN RIFLES OF CANADA, FOR ACTIONS JUNE 6, 1944, TO MAY 8, 1945

The Distinguished Service Order
Major H. Elliot Dalton
Major Richard D. Medland

The Military Cross
Lieutenant John E. Boos

The Distinguished Conduct Medal
Company Sergeant-Major Charles C. Martin

The Military Medal
Company Sergeant-Major Charles C. Martin DCM
Sergeant Charles W. Smith
Rifleman Charles Nahwegezhik
Rifleman J.M. Watson

Mentioned in Despatches
Major H. Elliot Dalton DSO
Major Donald Hogarth
Captain Peter C. Rea
Captain John L. Pond
Sgt. William A. Lennox
Corporal F.N. Brisebois

APPENDIX E
MEMBERS OF A COMPANY, THE QUEEN'S OWN
RIFLES, AS OF JUNE 3–6, 1944

This list was taken from a handwritten notebook prepared in England by George Dalzell before embarkation for the D-Day landing. Sample pages of the notebook are reproduced below. After Dalzell was killed on June 6, 1944, Charlie Martin kept his book. The full roster, as George prepared it, follows in text over the next several pages.

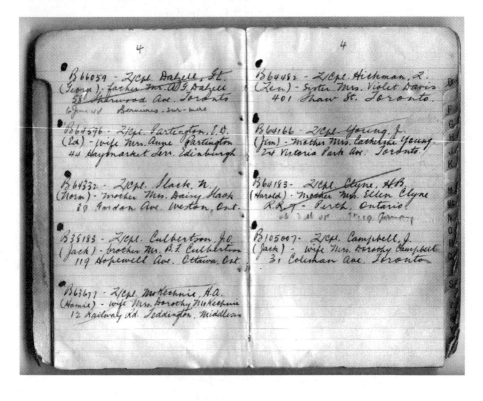

Alexander, J.A.S., Rfn.
68 King Street East
Chatham, Ontario

Allair, J.A., Rfn.
R. R. 8
Picton, Ontario

Allison, L., Rfn.
64 Borden Street
Toronto, Ontario

Andrews, G.F., Rfn.
42 Pickering Street
Toronto, Ontario

Ashton, E.L., Rfn.
4 Humbert Street
Toronto, Ontario

Attwater, F.M., Rfn.
43 Redpath Avenue
Toronto, Ontario

Bailey, D.R., Rfn.
6 North Street
Galt, Ontario

Beatty, L.E., Rfn.
531 Albert Street
Oshawa, Ontario

Bencharski, J., Rfn.
Ashville, Manitoba

Bennett, G.E., Rfn.
10 Byron Place
Staple Hill, Bristol, U.K.

Bennett, J.W., Cpl.
R. R. 1, Saulte Highway
Coppercliff, Ontario

Bettridge, W.G., Rfn.
6 Mill Street
Brampton, Ontario

Bland, J.M., Rfn.
474 Danforth Avenue
Toronto, Ontario

Bloomfield, C.M., Rfn.
1727 Dufferin Street
Toronto, Ontario

Bodie, R.G., Rfn.
408 - 5th Avenue East
Calgary, Alberta

Boyd, J.M., Rfn.
234 Charles Street
Belleville, Ontario

Briere, G.J., Rfn.
Albertville, Sask.

Brisebois, F.N., Rfn.
234 Leslie Street
Sudbury, Ontario

Brough, R.O., Rfn.
Highland Creek, Ontario

Brown, W., A/Cpl.
21 Carnation Avenue
Long Branch, Ontario

Browne, J.S., Sgt.
235 Thomson Dr.
Winnipeg, Manitoba

Bruyère, B., Rfn.
50 Lennox Street
Cornwall, Ontario

Bruyère, H.J., Rfn.
50 Lennox Street
Cornwall, Ontario

Buchanan, A.W., Rfn.
110 Millicent Street
Toronto, Ontario

Burnett, R.G., Rfn.
Echo Bay, Ontario

Campbell, J., L/Cpl.
31 Coleman Avenue
Toronto, Ontario

Carmichael, J.R.P., Rfn.
96 Caithness Avenue
Toronto, Ontario

Carr, W.H., Rfn.
c/o Rawson Institute
Bolney, Sussex, U.K.

Catling, J.R., Rfn.
R. R. 1
Echo Bay, Ontario

Chalmers, C.W., Rfn.
814A Bathurst Street
Toronto, Ontario

Clark, J.S., Rfn.
2301 St. Clair Avenue West
Toronto, Ontario

Clyne, H.B., L/Cpl.
R. R. 7
Perth, Ontario

Cole, G., Rfn.
Cache Bay Road
Sturgeon Falls, Ontario

Couroux, A., Rfn.
615 Keele Street
Toronto, Ontario

Culbertson, J.O., L/Cpl.
119 Hopewell Avenue
Ottawa, Ontario

Cunningham, E.A., Rfn.
24 Gillespie Avenue
Toronto, Ontario

Dalton, H.E., Major
141 Lawton Blvd.
Toronto, Ontario

Dalzell, G.L., L/Cpl.
58 Sharwood Avenue
Toronto, Ontario

Darby, J.J., Cpl.
1188 College Street
Toronto, Ontario

Davis, J.S., Rfn.
22 Elmer Avenue
Toronto, Ontario

Dawds, J.D.N., Rfn.
426 Delaware Avenue
Toronto, Ontario

deBlois, A.A., Rfn.
Box 429
Cochrane, Ontario

de Blois, E.L., Rfn.
149 Sumatra Road
Hampstead, London, NW6

de Blois, S., Rfn.
Box 429
Cochrane, Ontario

Dermody, G.E., A/Cpl.
Kennedy, Sask.

Doner, D.G., Rfn.
40 Cortland Avenue
Toronto, Ontario

Duggan, C.A., Rfn.
R. R. 1
Schomberg, Ontario

English, G., Rfn.
189 Dunraven Drive
Toronto, Ontario

Engstrom, J.A., Rfn.
69 Balsam Street North
Timmins, Ontario

Garrett, G.C., C.Q.M.S.
1642 North Main Street
Niagara Falls, Ontario

Giroux, M.J.E., Rfn.
193 Montreal Road
Eastview, Ontario

Grier, W., Rfn.
R. R. 2
Elmvale, Ontario

Gyatt, J., Rfn.
11 Nausch Road
Sparkhill, Birmingham, U.K.

Hackett, E.E., Rfn.
92 Methuen Avenue
Toronto, Ontario

Hall, S.J., Rfn.
11 Cadorna Avenue
Toronto, Ontario

Harber, T L., Rfn.
197 Hannah Street
Midland, Ontario

Harden, C.H., Rfn.
198 Croyden Road
Caterham Valley, Surrey

Haskins, W.J., Rfn.
Madawaska, Ontario

Hawkins, H.H., Rfn.
3 Mariposa Avenue
Toronto, Ontario

Hickman, L., L/Cpl.
401 Shaw Street
Toronto, Ontario

Hill, T.L., Rfn.
35 Belses Drive
Glasgow, Scotland SW2

Hill, W.H., Rfn.
22 Mary Street
Barrie, Ontario

Hindle, W.F.A., Rfn.
134 Glenforest Road
Toronto, Ontario

Kerr, J.T., Rfn.
154 Felstead Avenue
Toronto, Ontario

Klintworth, R.J., Rfn.
56 Lewis Street
Toronto, Ontario

Kushniryk, S., Rfn.
Bowsman River, Man.

Leather, J., Rfn.
16 Givins Street
Toronto, Ontario

Lennox, W.A., Cpl.
Apt. 5, 2 Grosvenor Street
Toronto, Ontario

Lindenas, N.E., Rfn.
Ridgeway, Ontario

Little, R.M., Rfn.
15 Brookside Drive
Toronto, Ontario

Lucas, E.J., Rfn.
Gravenhurst, Ontario

Marshall, R.A., Rfn.
225 Elgin Street
Brantford, Ontario

Martin, C.C., C.S.M.
16 Marx Terrace, Chapwell
Newcastle-on-Tyne, U.K.

May, W.G., Rfn.
65 Princess Road
London NW1, U.K.

McBride, W., Rfn.
84 Dunkirk Road
Toronto, Ontario

McCullough, R.F., Rfn.
Box 225
Newmarket, Ontario

McGregor, J., Rfn.
9 Little Blvd.
Toronto, Ontario

McKechnie, H.A., L/Cpl.
12 Railway Road
Teddington, Middlesex

McNab, P.D., Rfn.
370 Laurier Avenue West
Ottawa, Ontario

McVicar, J.A., Rfn.
23 Belses Drive
Glasgow SW2, Scotland

Meagher, J., Rfn.
Brook Village
Inverness, Nova Scotia

Medland, R.D., Capt.
63 Parkwood Avenue
Toronto, Ontario

Mercer, W.G., Rfn.
339 New Street/Jean Street
Orillia, Ontario

Mitchell, R.D., Rfn.
14 McLaughlin Blvd.
Oshawa, Ontario

Mitchell, W.M., Rfn.
340 Simcoe Street South
Oshawa, Ontario

Moore, J.R., Rfn.
6 Vivian Street
Toronto, Ontario

Morgan, J.F., Rfn.
94 Lyall Avenue
Toronto, Ontario

Morland, D., A/Cpl.
6 Main Street
Toronto, Ontario

Morrison, W.F., Rfn.
1014 Logan Avenue
Toronto, Ontario

Mumberson, F.M., Rfn.
61 West Street
Brampton, Ontario

Munro, J.B., Rfn.
24 Dorval Road
Toronto, Ontario

O'Brien, C., Rfn.
13^1/2 Gerrard Street West
Toronto, Ontario

Oliver, G.R.O., Rfn.
Division Street
Cobourg, Ontario

Overholt, W.A., Sgt.
70 Salisbury Avenue
Toronto, Ontario

Overy, J.J., Rfn.
30 Beaconsfield Avenue
Toronto, Ontario

Owen, D.D., Lieut.
186 Warren Road
Toronto, Ontario

Pallante, M., Rfn.
35 Ferry Street West
Hamilton, Ontario

Partington, E.W., L/Cpl.
44 Haymarket Terrace
Edinburgh, Scotland

Patterson, E., Rfn.
455 Bay Street North
Hamilton, Ontario

Payne, H., Cpl.
524 Greenwood Avenue
Toronto, Ontario

Payne, H.G., Rfn.
23 Gladstone Avenue
Toronto, Ontario

Penford, R.W., Rfn.
51 Libra Road
Plaistow, London E13, U.K.

Phelps, F.E.G., Rfn.
168 Elliott Avenue
Oshawa, Ontario

Pierce, L.J., Rfn.
15 Delaney Crescent
Toronto, Ontario

Pond, J.L., Lieut.
19 Benlamond Avenue
Toronto, Ontario

Rea, P.C., Lieut.
525 Russell Hill Road
Toronto, Ontario

Reid, R.C., Rfn.
147 Christie Street
Toronto, Ontario

Roberts, J.D., Rfn.
296 Milverton Blvd.
Toronto, Ontario

Rocks, H.M., A/Cpl.
31 Main Street
Kirkland Lake, Ontario

Ruttan, L.A., Rfn.
Stoneleight, Ontario

Sackfield, J.C., Rfn.
149 Sumatra Road
Hampstead, London NW6

Screen, E.R., L/Sgt.
36 Batavia Avenue
Toronto, Ontario

Shepperd, A.J., Rfn.
Apt. A, 243 Dovercourt Road
Toronto, Ontario

Simpson, J.M., L/Sgt.
194 Cottingham Street
Toronto, Ontario

Simpson, W.J., Rfn.
70 Pape Avenue
Toronto, Ontario

Slack, N., L/Cpl.
39 Gordon Avenue
Weston, Ontario

Smith, C.W., A/Sgt.
135 Banning Street
Port Arthur, Ontario

Smith, J.R., Rfn.
Box 236
Grimsby, Ontario

Stock, H., Rfn.
Bala, Ontario

Taylor, J.E., Rfn.
89 Ferrier Avenue
Toronto, Ontario

Taylor, W.C., Rfn.
364 Simcoe Street West, Apt. 4
Oshawa, Ontario

Twynam, T., Rfn.
82 Langford Avenue
Toronto, Ontario

Willis, S.G., Rfn.
60 Humber Blvd.
Toronto, Ontario

Yaffe, L., Rfn.

Young, J., L/Cpl.
24 Victoria Park Avenue
Toronto, Ontario

APPENDIX F
NOMINAL ROLE OF A COMPANY,
THE QUEEN'S OWN RIFLES,
AFTER REINFORCEMENT AND BEFORE THE
BATTLE OF THE SCHELDT

Reproduced on the next five pages is the list of the members of A Company before the battle of the Scheldt. A comparison with the list in Appendix E reveals just how many men were lost in the preceding months.

"A" Company   Nominal Roll of Next-of-Kin   Revised 29 Sept/44.

Regt'l No.	Rank	Name	N.of K.	Address of N.of K.
	A/Maj.	R.D. Medland	Mother	Mrs. E.J. Medland 63 Parkwood Ave., Toronto, Ont.
	Lieut.	J.L. Pond	Wife	Mrs. Helen Mary Pond 19 Benlomand Ave., Toront, Ont.
	Lieut.	J.E. Boos L.	Wife	Mrs. Theo Boose 52 Pepler Ave., Toronto, Ont.
	Lieut.	A.E. King	Mother	Mrs. H.W. King 4790 Cotes-des-Verge Rd., Montreal
	Lieut.	G. Hynes	Wife	Mrs. J.G.W. Haynes 495 Caledonia Rd., Toronto, Ont.
B63919	C.S.M.	Martin, C.C.	Wife	Mrs. Viole Martin 16 Marke Terr. Chopwell, Newcastle, Eng
B88324	CQMS	Garrett, G.C.	Wife	Mrs. Dorothy Garret 1642 Nth. Main St., Niagara Falls Ont
B63979	A/Sgt.	Lennox, W.A.	Wife	Mrs. Elsie Lennox 2 Grosvenor St., Apt. 5, Toronto, Ont.
B64179	A/Sgt.	Smith, C.W.	Mother	Mrs. Kate Soderquist 135 Banning St., Port Arthur, Ont.
B64176	A/Sgt.	Meagher, J.	Mother	Mrs. Katherine Meagher Brook Village, Inverness , N.S.
B64326	L/Sgt.	Bland, J.W.	Mother	Mrs. Agnes, Bland 474 Danforth Ave., Toronto, Ont.
B64837	Cpl.	Collins, F.A.	Wife	Mrs. Annie Collins R.R. No.2, Gormley, Ont.
B64479	Cpl.	Payne, H.	Father	Mr. Wm. Payne 524 Greenwood Ave., Toronto, Ont.
B127937	A/Cpl.	Kavanaugh, T.	Wife	Mrs. M.A. Kavanaugh 46 Wentworth St. N.Hamilton, Ont.
B126522	A/CPL.	Brisboise, F.K.	Mother	Mrs. Alexina Brisboise 254 Leslie St., Sudbury Ont.
B48793	A/Cpl.	Cooper, P.J.	Wife	Mrs. Mary, J. Cooper 560 Armour Rd., Peterborough, Ont.
B114006	A/Cpl.	Allison, L.	Wife	Mrs. Madeline Allison 1058 Shaw, St., Toronto, Ont.
B41776	I/Cpl.	Keeton, H.S.	Wife	Mrs. A. Keeton 422 Wellington St., S. Hamilton, Ont.
B64148	L/Cpl.	Twynam, T.	Mother	Mrs. Rose May Twynam 82 Langford Ave., Toronto, Ont.
B117606	L/Cpl.	Antonese, G.	Brother	Mrs.Wm. Antonese 2492a Denontegnye, Montreal, Que.
F9426	L/Cpl.	Dunphy, W.J.	Mother	Mrs. F. Dunphy Head Chezzethook, Hfx. N.S.
B135174	L/Cpl.	Jones, E.L.	Mother	Mrs. Susan Jones 502 Concession St., Hamilton, Ont.
B135938	L/Cpl.	Pennell, W.G.	Mother	Mrs. Geraldine Pennell 958 Dundas St., E., Toronto, Ont.
C121594	L/Cpl.	McNab, P.O.	Wife	Mrs
B45176	L/Cpl.	Boyd, J.W.	Mother	Mrs. Mae Boyd 2,4 Charles St., Belleville, Ont.

"A" Coy.		Nominal Roll of Next-Of-Kin (2)		Revised 29 Sept/44
Regt'l No.	Rank	Name	N.of K.	Address of N. of K.
B24260	L/Cpl.	Leather, J.	Wife	Mrs. Mary Leather 76 Givens St., Toronto, Ont.
B22764	Rfn.	Archibald T.	Father	Mr. Sidney Wm. Archibald Island Falls Junction, Ont.
B131294	Rfn.	Atkinson E. H.	Mother	Mrs. Nellie Atkinson 51 Grandville Ave., Mount Dennis, Ont.
D136615	Rfn.	Atto J. W.	Father	Mr. Harold Lynn Atto 1540 Summerhill Ave., Apt. 8. Montreal.Qu.
B46512	Rfn.	Aussem, H.	Father	Mr. Bert Aussem 14 Tisdale St., South Hamilton, Ont.
B149010	Rfn.	bBarrett, A.	Wife	Mrs. Elizabeth Barrett 188 Woodville, Ave., Toronto, Ont.
C112142	Rfn.	Barrett, J.M.	Mother	Mrs. E.Barrett 118 Pinnacle St., Belleville, Ont.
B158986	Rfn.	Beardshaw, G.H.	Mother	Mrs. Mary E.Beardshaw C/O Mrs. Flynn. 24 Crabtree Rd. Densc-roft Yorks, Eng
B65834	Rfn.	Beatty, L.E.	Wife	Mrs. Winnifred Beatty 531 Albert St., Ottowa,'Ont
C118591	Rfn.	Bird, I.H.	Mother	Mrs. I Bird R.R. No. JR Janetville, Ont.
B127918	Rfn.	Bloomfield, C.M.	Mother	Mrs. Clara Bloomfield 1727 Dufferin St., Toronto, Ont.
A114071	Rfn.	Boose, H.W.	Wife	Mrs. H.W. Boose New Canaan P.O., Ont.
B156798	Rfn.	Borman, L.A.	Mother	Mrs. Nora Borman 45 Fisher St., Kitchener, Ont.
M38822	Rfn.	Bragg, H.T.	Mother	Mrs. Mary Bragg R.R. No. 3. Ponoka, Alta.
B132200	Rfn.	Bridge, G.	Sister	Mrs. Katherline Barrow 533 Hughston St., North Hamilton, Ont -
B64725	Rfn.	Brough, R.O.	Grandmother	Mrs. Annie Smith Highland, Creek, Ont.
L91715	Rfn.	Brown, R.A.	Wife	Mrs. R.A. Brown 640 3rds Ave. Swift Current, Ont.
B20026	Rfn.	Bradburn, W.	Wife	Mrs. C.Bradburn 4024 Leage St., Verdun P.C, Que.
B55641	Rfn.	Brunet, G.A.	Mother	Mrs. A Bertran Connaught Ont.
C31400	Rfn.	Bruyere, E.	Mother	Mrs. Dora Bruyere 50 Lennox St., Cornwall, Ont.
H69865	Rfn.	Burke, O.R.	Father	Mr. Harry Burke Upsala, Ont.
B158458	Rfn.	Carlton, S.C.	Mother	Mrs. Mary Anne Carlton 8 Lawrence St., Parry Sound, Ont.
B126528	Rfn.	Cargill, L.E.	Mother	Mr. Thos.Berrt R.R. No. 3 Milton, Ont.
C52681	Rfn.	Cosgrove, W.G.	Father	Mr. Harry Cosgrove 25 Hannah St., Eastview, Ont.
K514663	Rfn.	Carrier, D.	Father	Mr. D. Carrier St. Paul, Ont.

"A" Coy 90 Nominal Roll of Next-of-Kin (4) Revised 29 Sept/44.

Regt'l No.	Rank	Name	N. of K.	Address of N. of K.
B115695	Rfn.	Harrop, E.D.	Father	Mr. Fredrick Harrop Debbie, Ont.
A104803	Rfn.	Hewitt, W.S.	Mother	Mrs. Gertrude Hewitt R-E, 1 Petrolia, Ont., Can.
B76006	Rfn.	Hauch, R.J.M.	Mother	Mrs. Clayton, Hauch 77 Pepler, St., Toronto, Ont.
B148552	Rfn.	Joslin, W.G.	Mother	Mrs. Jean Joslin Barrie Rd. E., Orrilia, Ont.
B64745	Rfn.	Kerr, J.T.	Mother	Mrs. aAlice Kerr 154 Felstead Ave., Toronto, Ont.
B103328	Rfn.	Kehoe, J.A.	Mother	Mrs. Katherine Kehoe R.R. 1 Bar River, Ont.
B63766	Rfn.	Klintworth, R.J.	Mother,	Mrs. Jane Klintworth 56 Lewis St., Toronto, Ont.
C58260	Rfn.	Leskie, L.	Aunt	Mrs. Margaret Vincent 44 Victoria St., Arnprior, Ont.
B133209	Rfn.	La Fontaine, F.S.	Mother	Mrs. Blanche LaFontaine 26 O'Brien St., North Bay, Ont.
B116773	Rfn.	McCoy, R.W.	Mother	Mrs. V. McCoy Seagrave, Ont.
C6348	Rfn.	McManus, J.J.	Wife	Mrs. Anna McManus 2 Renfrew Way, Renfrew, Ont.
C103503	Rfn.	Malone, A.E.	Mother	Mrs. C. Malone Box 878 Nassua, N.P. B.W.I. Bahamas.
B142625	Rfn.	Mannard, N.R.	Mother	Mrs. J. Mannard 2186 Jacques Hertlem St., Montreal, Que.
B136965	Rfn.	Morgan, J.F.	Mother	Mrs. J.F. Morgan 94 Lyall Ave., Toronto, Ont.
B52575	Rfn.	Naweghzhik, C.	Father	Mr. Charles Nakwegezhik Shequiandah, Ont.
B119213	Rfn.	Ninnis, G.W.	Wife	Mrs. Terrace Ninnis Allanburg, Ont.
B64297	Rfn.	O'Brien, C.	Mother	Mrs. B. O'Brien 1312 Gerrard St., W., Toronto, Ont.
B149284	Rfn.	Overland, D.R.	Mother	Mrs. Lena Overland Warkgo, Sask.
D143197	Rfn.	Page, L.G.	Mother	Mrs. Mary Page Calumet, Que.
F57585	Rfn.	Paul, J.N.	Mother	Mrs. Joseph Paul Hequille Annapolis, Co. N.S.
F3489	Rfn.	Parsons, L.E.	Brother	Mr. G.P. Parsons Box 450 Renfrew, Ont.
B68020	Rfn.	Penford, R.W.	Wife	Mrs. Dorothy Penford 51 Lebra Rd., Plaistow, London, E. 13
B117100	Rfn.	Robinson, L.W.	Wife	Mrs. R. Robinson Box 328 Beeton, Ont.
B118763	Rfn.	Rowe, F.	Wife	Mrs. Margaret Rowe Little Current, Ont.
B116162	Rfn.	Riddell, J.A.	Mother	Mrs. Lily Riddell 34 Wadeworth St., Brantford, Ont.
G1979	Rfn.	Ryan, E.J.	Mother	Mrs. Jane Ryan Humphries Mill, N.S. Can.

Nominal Roll of Next-of-Kin (5) Revised 29 Sept/44.

Regt'l No.	Rank	Name	N.ofK.	Adress of N. O. K.
B16667	Rfn.	Caverly, A.T.	Mother	Mary Emma Caverly Whitney, Ont.
B21859	Rfn.	Chadwick, J.	Mother	Mrs. Mary Chadwick 22 Wallon Ave., Toronto, Ont.
B74174	Rfn.	Chalmers, C.W.	Wife	Mrs. Cary Chalmers 814a Bathurst St., Toronto, Ont.
B98010	Rfn.	Chapman, R.E.	Sister	Mrs. Violet Pearl Pyatt R.R. 5, Hamilton, Ont.
H69954	Rfn.	Charlet, E.	Father	Mr. Ka Charlet 365 Salter St. Winipeg, Man.
B126521	Rfn.	Clark, A.	Father	Mr. Arthur Clark R.R. No. 2, Lowbanks, Ont.
B44947	Rfn.	Cleary, L.M.	Father	Mr. Dan. C.eary 1304 College St., Toronto, Ont.
B17801	Rfn.	Chiblow, C.	Mother	Mrs. Mary Chiblow Blind River, Ont.
B17885	Rfn.	Chilton, J.W.	Wife	Mrs. Mary Chilton 382 Bathurst St., Toronto. Ont.
B83333	Rfn.	Coureux, A.	Father	Mr. Antoine Coureux 515 Keele St., Toronto, Ont.
B98079	Rf.	Cuthbert, J.W.	Mother	Mrs. Helen Cuthbert 54 Merritt St., Merriton, Ont.
B63547	Rfn.	Darby, J.J.	Mother	Mrs. Mary Darby 1188 College St., Toronto, Ont.
B57496	Rfn.	Dent, T.B.	Mother	Mrs. A. Dent 17 Huron St., Hamilton, Ont.
H102499	Rfn.	Drake, D.	Father	Mr. J. Drake Armstrong, Ont.
F9473	Rfn.	Drew, R.K.	Mother	Mrs. Laura Drew Terrence Bay, Halifax, N.S.
B91884	Rfn.	Dunstan, W.R.	Wife	Mrs. Gwen Dunstan 50 Kennedy Ave., Toronto, Ont.
J64740	Rfn.	Eby, L.D.	Mother	Mrs. Teresa Eby 1041 McMillan Ave., Winnipeg, Man.
B74592	Rfn.	Engstrom J.A	Mother	Mrs Eleanor Engstrom 69 Balsam St., North Timmins, Ont.
A114009	Rfn.	Fraser, C.	Brother	Mrs Lorne Fraser 357 Edmonton St., London, Ont.
B46527	Rfn.	Freelen, E.J.	Mother	Mrs. Anne Freelen Balsover, Ont.
B142883	Rfn.	Gardner, J.E	Father	Mr. D. Gardner 64 Golfview Ave., Toronto, Ont.
D7.318	Rfn.	Gardiner, L.L.	Mother	Mrs. E.Gardiner R.R. No. 5 Perth, Ont.
B63510	Rfn.	Goldenthal, S.	Mother	Mrs. Sophie Goldenthal 144 Major St., Toronto, Ont.
B64910	Rfn.	Grier, W.	Mother	Mrs. Agnes Grier C/O Mrs. Esher Graham R.R. 2 Elmville, Ont
A107892	Rfn.	Griffin, R.J.	Mother	Mrs. E. Griffin 847 Eugene St., Windsor

"A" Coy.   Nominal Roll of Next-of-Kin   (5) Revised 29 Sept/44.

Regt'l No.	Rank	Name	N. of K.	Address of N. of K.
D141399	Rfn.	Saunders, D.P.	Sister	Mrs. Alice Downey 1714 St. James St, W. Montreal, Que.
D138928	Rfn.	Sawka, H.	Father	Mr. Mike Sawka 718 12th. St. Nrth Lethbridge, Alta.
B63787	Rfn.	Simpson, J.H.	Mother	Mrs. Florence Simpson 3 East Avenue, Waterside Londenderry, North Ireland.
B143758	Rfn.	Schram, R.G.	Mother	Mrs. W. Schram Victoria, Ont.
B63870	Rfn.	Smith, J.R.	Mother	Mrs. J. Smith Box 236 Grimsbsby, Ont.
G34925	Rfn.	Steeves, P.F.	Mother	Mrs. Alice Steeves Edgetts Landing Alberts Cty., N.B.
B158651	Rfn.	Tilley, J.A.	Mother	Mrs. L.Tilley 224 Grosvenor St., Nrth. Hamilton, Ont.
B116569	Rfn.	Warner, G.R.	Mother	Mrs. G. Warner 21 Marmott St., Toronto, Ont.
C23288	Rfn.	Watson, W.H.	Mother	Mrs. F. Watson. Norland, Ont.
B40593	Rfn.	West, H.G.	Mother	Mrs. Pearl West 370 Thoroldstone Rd. Niagar Falls, Ont.
B64065	Rfn.	Welch, W.	Sister	Mrs. E.G. Cordner 2291 Dundas St., W. Toronto, Ont.
B131997	Rfn.	Wilson, H.W.	Brother	Mrs. Glen Wilson Box 430 Renfrew, Ont.
A109068	Rfn.	Wood, C.L.	Wife	Mrs. A.Wood 9950 Minnock St., Detroit 23 Mich., U.S.A.

CANADA REMEMBERS
LE CANADA SE SOUVIENT

A national program commemorating the 50th anniversary of the end of the Second World War

Logo: The maple leaf in gold symbolizes the country Canada celebrating the 50th anniversary of the end of the Second World War. The foreground poppy is in remembrance of those Canadians who served and died overseas, and the background poppy commemorates those who lost their lives in Canada and reminds us of the wives, husbands, children and all those who played a vital supporting role at home. The intertwining of the three elements symbolizes the unity and strength of Canadians and their loyalty, dedication and sacrifice – enduring values that will sustain Canada in the future.